The New York Times

LOOKING FORWARD

Net Neutrality

SEEKING A FREE AND FAIR INTERNET

THE NEW YORK TIMES EDITORIAL STAFF

Published in 2019 by New York Times Educational Publishing
in association with The Rosen Publishing Group, Inc.
29 East 21st Street, New York, NY 10010

First Edition

The New York Times
Alex Ward: Editorial Director, Book Development
Heidi Giovine: Administrative Manager
Phyllis Collazo: Photo Rights/Permissions Editor
Brenda Hutchins: Senior Photo Editor/Art Buyer

Rosen Publishing
Jacob R. Steinberg: Director of Content Development
Greg Tucker: Creative Director
Brian Garvey: Art Director

Cataloging-in-Publication Data
Names: New York Times Company.
Title: Net neutrality: seeking a free and fair internet / edited by the New York Times editorial staff.
Description: New York : New York Times Educational Publishing, 2019. | Series: Looking forward | Includes bibliographic references and index.
Identifiers: ISBN 9781642820898 (pbk.) | ISBN 9781642820904 (library bound) | ISBN 9781642820911 (ebook)
Subjects: LCSH: Network neutrality—Juvenile literature. | Internet governance—Juvenile literature. | Telecommunication policy—Juvenile literature.
Classification: LCC HE7645.N464 2019 | DDC 384.3'3—dc23

Manufactured in the United States of America

On the cover: People hold signs supporting net neutrality at a rally with members of Congress outside the Capitol in Washington on Feb. 27, 2018; Erin Schaff for The New York Times.

Contents

Introduction

WHEN THE WORLD WIDE WEB was invented, its creator, Sir Tim Berners-Lee, envisioned a global platform on which all users would have the ability to communicate and share information on equal footing. It was in 1989, while working as a scientist at the European Organization for Nuclear Research, or CERN, that Sir Tim initially proposed creating such an information-sharing system.

Sir Tim's web was to host "hypertext," that is, documents in which links to other documents were embedded into readable text for ease of reference. The web would be the graphic interface necessary to allow users to share information over the internet, an existing global network of various computer networks.

Within a year of his proposal, work was underway to create the web. Integral to Sir Tim's vision was the idea that all users could both read and create hypertext documents. This component made the World Wide Web a truly democratic medium, an open platform to which any user with a computer could connect to send and receive information.

After Sir Tim's web browser was released to the public in 1991, few challenged this notion that the web should remain open and decentralized, allowing users unfettered access to any content transmitted over the internet. In fact, most users took it for granted.

Yet, since the early 2000s, telecommunications companies have threatened the democratic nature of the web. Detecting an opportunity for profit, many internet service providers began proposing new, tiered systems of access. Major corporations that could afford to pay more would have the opportunity to have their emails and data reach users at a premium speed, while small businesses that could not afford it would likely get shut out by the competition.

DANIEL ROSENBAUM FOR THE NEW YORK TIMES

Protesters in favor of net neutrality at the Federal Communications Commission's headquarters on Thursday, May 15, 2014, before the F.C.C. panel voted to open for public debate rules on net neutrality.

In 2007, Verizon Wireless attempted to block the text messages of Naral Pro-Choice America, an abortion rights group, from being sent over its mobile network. In the face of public outrage, Verizon stood down, blaming a misapplication of internal policy. In 2010, Sprint Nextel interfered in Catholic Relief Services' efforts to employ a call-to-text program to solicit donations using its network. In that case, Sprint blamed incomplete paperwork required to verify the charity's legitimacy.

Both cases highlighted an important reality: There were no clear guidelines outlining the Federal Communication Commission's role in regulating new, quickly growing telecommunications mediums such as text messaging or emails. At best, internal policy and red tape might interfere with users' communications. At worst, telecom companies were ripe for censorship and the intentional blocking of information.

In 2003, Columbia University law professor Tim Wu coined the term "network neutrality," or "net neutrality" for short. The idea was simple:

The telecommunications companies who control the infrastructure of the internet should not be able to restrict how customers use it.

Wu's concept described how the web had, de facto, worked since its creation 14 years prior. However, as internet service providers explored the possibility of delivering faster data for those companies that could pay for it and of enabling or preventing users from accessing certain types of content contingent upon their ability to afford it, net neutrality appeared threatened.

This is the groundwork for a debate that continues to this day over whether or not net neutrality should be the guiding principle behind internet access and what role government agencies should play in enforcing such a principle.

Detractors of net neutrality argue that telecommunications companies invested in building the network and so they should have some right to regulate what passes through it. Furthermore, they point to the reward of greater profit as the motivation these companies need to develop better, more reliable systems for data delivery.

However, defenders hearken to Sir Tim's original vision for the web, defining the internet as a basic utility that all users should have the ability to use freely to access the data and content they wish at an equal rate of speed. In Sir Tim's own words, "the neutrality of the Net is a medium essential for democracy."

With the shift of administrations — and political agendas — there have been changes in the F.C.C.'s policies on net neutrality. Under the Obama administration, the F.C.C. pushed back against courts and legislators to develop net neutrality rules that would stick.

Now, however, the future of net neutrality is uncertain. Ajit Pai, F.C.C. chair since 2017, has spearheaded the end of previously enacted F.C.C. regulations. Meanwhile, states, legislators and citizens have stepped forward to defend the democratic nature of the internet.

CHAPTER 1

The Early Days of Net Neutrality

In the early days of the net neutrality debate, advocates argued that the Internet was a utility, and as such, telecom companies had no right to hinder the delivery of data transmitted over it. Critics, however, maintained that these companies had, at their own expense, built the "pipes" of the network and so they had the right to charge premium rates for faster speeds to repay their investment and foster further innovation. As companies explored new practices that violated net neutrality, calls for clear regulatory guidelines increased and the public took notice of the issue.

Hey, Baby Bells: Information Still Wants to Be Free

BY RANDALL STROSS | JAN. 15, 2006

AT THE TOP of my wish list for next year's Consumer Electronics Show is this: the introduction of broadband service across the country that is as up to date as that 103-inch flat-screen monitor just introduced by Panasonic. The digital lifestyle I see portrayed so alluringly in ads is not possible when the Internet plumbing in our homes is as pitiful as it is. The broadband carriers that we have today provide service that attains negative perfection: low speeds at high prices.

It gets worse. Now these same carriers — led by Verizon Communications and BellSouth — want to create entirely new categories of fees that risk destroying the anyone-can-publish culture of the Internet. And they are lobbying for legislative protection of their meddling with the Internet content that runs through their pipes. These are not good ideas.

Slow broadband seems to be our cursed lot. Until we get an upgrade — or rather an upgrade to an upgrade — the only Americans who will enjoy truly fast and inexpensive service will be those who leave the country. In California, Comcast cable broadband provides top download speeds of 6 megabits a second for a little more than $50 a month. That falls well short, however, of Verizon's 15-megabit fiber-based service offered on the East Coast at about the same price. But what about the 100-megabit service in Japan for $25 month? And better, much better: Stockholm's one-gigabit service — that is, 1,000 megabits, or more than 1,300 times faster than Verizon's entry-level DSL service — for less than 100 euros, or $120, a month.

One-gigabit service is not in the offing in the United States. What the network carriers seem most determined to sell is a premium form of Internet service that offers a tantalizing prospect of faster, more reliable delivery — but only if providers like Google, Yahoo and Microsoft pay a new charge for special delivery of their content. (That charge, by the way, would be in addition to the regular bandwidth-based Internet connection charges that their carriers already levy.)

An executive vice president of Verizon, for example, said last week that the proliferation of video programs offered via the Internet opens a new opportunity for his company: a new class of premium online delivery for Web sites wishing to pay extra to give smooth video streams to their customers in the Verizon service area. The executive, Thomas J. Tauke, said that a fast lane for premium content providers would not reduce the quality of regular service for everyone else, and that sites could choose not to sign up without suffering retribution. "To the best of my knowledge," he said, "there's no negative."

From the consumer's perspective, given the dismal state of the status quo, shouldn't any service improvement be welcomed? The short answer is: not necessarily.

For one thing, the occasional need for a preferential fast lane for streaming video — that is, moving pictures displayed as fast as they arrive, rather than downloaded first and played from memory — exists in the United States only because our standard broadband speeds are so slow. Were we ever to become a nation with networks supporting gigabit service, streaming video would not require special handling.

Perhaps more important, the superabundance of content in the Internet's ecosystem is best explained by its organizing principle of "network neutrality." The phrase refers to the way the Internet welcomes everyone who wishes to post content. Consumers, in turn, enjoy limitless choices. Rather than having network operators select content providers on our behalf — the philosophy of the local cable company — the Internet allows all of us to act as our own network programmers, serving a demographic of just one person.

Today, the network carrier has a minor, entirely neutral role in this system — providing the pipe for the bits that move the last miles to the home. It has no say about where those bits happened to have originated. Any proposed change in its role should be examined carefully, especially if the change entails expanding the carrier's power to pick and choose where bits come from — a power that has the potential to abrogate network neutrality.

This should be taken into account when Baby Bells say they need to extract more revenue from their networks in order to finance service improvements. Consumers will pay one way or the other, whether directly, as Internet access fees, or indirectly, as charges when a content company opts for special delivery and passes along its increased costs to its customers. It would be better for the network carriers to continue to do as they have, by charging higher rates for higher bandwidth. (Sign me up for that one-gigabit service.)

Left unmentioned in Verizon's pitch is the concentration of power that it enjoys in its service area, which would allow it to ignore the equal-access principle whenever it wishes. We are asked to take on faith that it and the other telephone companies with similar plans will

JUSTIN FINES

handle ordinary network traffic with the same care they would show if they had not begun parallel businesses for the carriage trade. How likely is that?

Vinton G. Cerf has as good a claim as anyone to being the "father" of the Internet — he was the co-author in the 1970's of key protocols that define it. He worked for many years at MCI and joined Google last year. After hearing a description of Verizon's contemplated offering of a premium delivery service for video, he was skeptical that Verizon and other broadband carriers would adhere to promises to keep their networks open.

Mr. Cerf said that back in the 1990's, when the Web arrived, consumers could choose from among hundreds of dial-up service providers, without geographical constraints. But "as broadband developed," he added, "the set of choices telescoped to zero, one or two," and the lack of choice means that "we now have a serious issue on our hands."

Woe to us all if the Internet's content is limited by the companies who also handle the plumbing. "The Future of Ideas," by Lawrence Lessig (Random House, 2001), shows how innovation and creativity associated with the Internet are the byproducts of its openness, its role as a commons that is accessible, by design, to all. Professor Lessig, who teaches law at Stanford, said last week that even now, broadband carriers have failed to demonstrate their commitment to the principle of network neutrality. "They've fought it at each stage," he said, "and they have never embraced the principle."

An illustration of his point popped up the same day. In an interview, William L. Smith, the chief technology officer at BellSouth, described to me his company's trial offering in West Palm Beach, Fla., last year of a speedy download service for Movielink content. When asked whether BellSouth would offer its special service on an exclusive basis to a particular content site and agree to exclude the sponsor's rivals, he did not hesitate in treating the question as a matter of simply settling on the right price. The N.F.L. and Nascar strike exclusive distribution deals, he said. Why not network carriers?

The largest Internet companies are the ones that could easily afford whatever terms the carriers demand for exclusive deals that would lock out smaller rivals and new entrants. But they have not done special deals with the carriers and instead have joined together to try to persuade Congress to protect the principle of network neutrality and prevent the Bells from striking exclusive deals with anyone. Last November, Amazon, eBay, Microsoft and Google, among others, formally registered their concern with a House committee that is revising the basic telecommunications law; they noted that a draft version of the bill failed to make network neutrality a matter of policy without exception. Whether the committee has responded positively to the suggestions from the Internet players should be known soon.

In his debut keynote address at the Consumer Electronics Show two weeks ago, one of Google's founders, Larry Page, credited the "dreamers in universities" who had had the foresight to create a network system without gatekeepers, which made it "maximally flexible" to permit the unplanned appearance of the World Wide Web. That, in turn, had made possible the unplanned appearance of Google.

More unplanned appearances will follow — but only if the ecosystem is protected from tromping telephone companies that are genetically incapable of understanding "maximally flexible."

RANDALL STROSS IS A HISTORIAN AND AUTHOR BASED IN SILICON VALLEY.

Tollbooths on the Internet Highway

OPINION | BY THE NEW YORK TIMES | FEB. 20, 2006

WHEN YOU USE THE INTERNET today, your browser glides from one Web site to another, accessing all destinations with equal ease. That could change dramatically, however, if Internet service providers are allowed to tilt the playing field, giving preference to sites that pay them extra and penalizing those that don't.

The Senate held hearings last week on "network neutrality," the principle that I.S.P.'s — the businesses like Verizon or Roadrunner that deliver the Internet to your computer — should not be able to stack the deck in this way. If the Internet is to remain free, and freely evolving, it is important that neutrality legislation be passed.

In its current form, Internet service operates in the same nondiscriminatory way as phone service. When someone calls your home, the telephone company puts through the call without regard to who is calling. In the same way, Internet service providers let Web sites operated by eBay, CNN or any other company send information to you on an equal footing. But perhaps not for long. It has occurred to the service providers that the Web sites their users visit could be a rich new revenue source. Why not charge eBay a fee for using the Internet connection to conduct its commerce, or ask Google to pay when customers download a video? A Verizon Communications executive recently sent a scare through cyberspace when he said at a telecommunications conference, as The Washington Post reported, that Google "is enjoying a free lunch" that ought to be going to providers like Verizon.

The solution, as far as the I.S.P.'s are concerned, could be what some critics are calling "access tiering," different levels of access for different sites, based on ability and willingness to pay. Giants like Walmart.com could get very fast connections, while little-guy sites might have to settle for the information superhighway equivalent of a one-lane, pothole-strewn road. Since many companies that own I.S.P.'s, like

Time Warner, are also in the business of selling online content, they could give themselves an unfair advantage over their competition.

If access tiering takes hold, the Internet providers, rather than consumers, could become the driving force in how the Internet evolves. Those corporations' profit-driven choices, rather than users' choices, would determine which sites and methodologies succeed and fail. They also might be able to stifle promising innovations, like Internet telephony, that compete with their own business interests.

Most Americans have little or no choice of broadband I.S.P.'s, so they would have few options if those providers shifted away from neutrality. Congress should protect access to the Internet in its current form. Senator Ron Wyden, an Oregon Democrat, says he intends to introduce an Internet neutrality bill, which would prohibit I.S.P.'s from favoring content providers that paid them fees, or from giving priority to their own content.

Some I.S.P.'s are phone and cable companies that make large campaign contributions, and are used to getting their way in Washington. But Americans feel strongly about an open and free Internet. Net neutrality is an issue where the public interest can and should trump the special interests.

No Neutral Ground in Net Debate

BY DAN MITCHELL | MAY 13, 2006

ACCORDING TO ARIANNA HUFFINGTON, the use of banal, insipid language could spell doom for the Internet.

It is not badly written blogs Ms. Huffington is worried about, but the concept "Net neutrality." Congress is debating whether to block Internet service providers from favoring some content providers over others. So, in theory, Time Warner or Verizon could prefer Yahoo over Google, or vice versa (or either of those over an upstart) by giving them more bandwidth in exchange for cash. The preferred sites would then run faster on PC's than those that do not pay.

Last week, Representative Edward J. Markey, Democrat of Massachusetts, introduced the Network Neutrality Act of 2006, a bill backed by Amazon, Microsoft and other Web companies, as well as disparate interests like the Gun Owners of America and the liberal group MoveOn.org. Proposed legislation that could change the nature of how the Internet operates should be getting a lot more attention, Ms. Huffington wrote. And if it did, it would be instantly squashed.

Why hasn't this happened? It's all in the name, she wrote. "Now, I understand that 'Net Neutrality' is a technical term used to describe the separation of content and network operations, but what political genius decided to run with such a clunky name? The marketing mavens behind the Kerry '04 campaign?"

The Huffington Post (huffingtonpost.com) has become a clearinghouse for debate. Most contributors are in favor of Net neutrality. But the site has also included arguments from, for example, Mike McCurry, the former Clinton press secretary who is chairman of Hands Off the Internet, a group financed by AT&T, BellSouth and other concerns and interest groups. The group calls itself "a nationwide coalition of Internet users" who oppose government regulation.

ALEX EBEN MEYER

On Huffington, Adam Green of MoveOn.org enumerated what he called lies from Mr. McCurry — for example, that the Internet was currently "absent regulation" and that a neutrality law would alter the way the Internet operates. Mr. Green argued that the Net was already neutral, and it was the telecom companies that wanted that to change.

Mr. McCurry decried the "culture and discourse of the Internet," referring to his detractors as "net neuts."

The telecom industry, he wrote, just wants the Net to be governed by economics, not government regulation. “Anyone want to have a rational conversation about that or do you want to rant and rave and provide a lot of May Day rhetoric that is not based in any fact?”

Why the Democratic Ethic of the World Wide Web May Be About to End

OPINION | BY ADAM COHEN | MAY 28, 2006

THE WORLD WIDE WEB is the most democratic mass medium there has ever been. Freedom of the press, as the saying goes, belongs only to those who own one. Radio and television are controlled by those rich enough to buy a broadcast license. But anyone with an Internet-connected computer can reach out to a potential audience of billions.

This democratic Web did not just happen. Sir Tim Berners-Lee, the British computer scientist who invented the Web in 1989, envisioned a platform on which everyone in the world could communicate on an equal basis. But his vision is being threatened by telecommunications and cable companies, and other Internet service providers, that want to impose a new system of fees that could create a hierarchy of Web sites. Major corporate sites would be able to pay the new fees, while little-guy sites could be shut out.

Sir Tim, who keeps a low profile, has begun speaking out in favor of "net neutrality," rules requiring that all Web sites remain equal on the Web. Corporations that stand to make billions if they can push tiered pricing through have put together a slick lobbying and marketing campaign. But Sir Tim and other supporters of net neutrality are inspiring growing support from Internet users across the political spectrum who are demanding that Congress preserve the Web in its current form.

The Web, which Sir Tim invented as a scientist at CERN, the European nuclear physics institute, is often confused with the Internet. But like e-mail, the Web runs over the system of interconnected computer networks known as the Internet. Sir Tim created the Web in a decentralized way that allowed anyone with a computer to connect to it and begin receiving and sending information.

That open architecture is what has allowed for the extraordinary growth of Internet commerce and communication. Pierre Omidyar, a small-time programmer working out of his home office, was able to set up an online auction site that anyone in the world could reach — which became eBay. The blogging phenomenon is possible because individuals can create Web sites with the World Wide Web prefix, www, that can be seen by anyone with Internet access.

Last year, the chief executive of what is now AT&T sent shock waves through cyberspace when he asked why Web sites should be able to "use my pipes free." Internet service providers would like to be able to charge Web sites for access to their customers. Web sites that could not pay the new fees would be accessible at a slower speed, or perhaps not be accessible at all.

A tiered Internet poses a threat at many levels. Service providers could, for example, shut out Web sites whose politics they dislike. Even if they did not discriminate on the basis of content, access fees would automatically marginalize smaller, poorer Web sites.

Consider online video, which depends on the availability of higher-speed connections. Internet users can now watch channels, like BBC World, that are not available on their own cable systems, and they have access to video blogs and Web sites like YouTube.com, where people upload videos of their own creation. Under tiered pricing, Internet users might be able to get videos only from major corporate channels.

Sir Tim expects that there are great Internet innovations yet to come, many involving video. He believes people at the scene of an accident — or a political protest — will one day be able to take pictures with their cellphones that could be pieced together to create a three-dimensional image of what happened. That sort of innovation could be blocked by fees for the high-speed connections required to relay video images. The companies fighting net neutrality have been waging a misleading campaign, with the slogan "hands off the Internet," that tries to look like a grass-roots effort to protect the Internet in its current form. What they actually favor is stopping the government from protecting the Internet, so they can get their own hands on it.

But the other side of the debate has some large corporate backers, too, like Google and Microsoft, which could be hit by access fees since they depend on the Internet service providers to put their sites on the Web. It also has support from political groups of all persuasions. The president of the Christian Coalition, which is allied with Moveon.org on this issue, recently asked, "What if a cable company with a pro-choice board of directors decides that it doesn't like a pro-life organization using its high-speed network to encourage pro-life activities?"

Forces favoring a no-fee Web have been gaining strength. One group, Savetheinternet.com, says it has collected more than 700,000 signatures on a petition. Last week, a bipartisan bill favoring net neutrality, sponsored by James Sensenbrenner, Republican of Wisconsin, and John Conyers Jr., Democrat of Michigan, won a surprisingly lopsided vote in the House Judiciary Committee.

Sir Tim argues that service providers may be hurting themselves by pushing for tiered pricing. The Internet's extraordinary growth has been fueled by the limitless vistas the Web offers surfers, bloggers and downloaders. Customers who are used to the robust, democratic Web may not pay for one that is restricted to wealthy corporate content providers.

"That's not what we call Internet at all," says Sir Tim. "That's what we call cable TV."

'Neutrality' Is New Challenge for Internet Pioneer

BY JOHN MARKOFF | SEPT. 27, 2006

SIR TIM BERNERS-LEE was a software programmer working at the CERN physics research laboratory in Switzerland in the 1980's when he proposed the idea of a project based on hypertext — linking documents with software pointers.

The World Wide Web went online in 1991 and rapidly grew beyond the physics community. In 1994, Sir Tim founded the World Wide Web Consortium at the Massachusetts Institute of Technology to promote open standards on the Internet. Earlier this year, he began speaking out in favor of "Net neutrality." The term describes one side in the debate in the United States over whether Internet service providers should be able to control the order in which they route packets of data — or even be able to reject those packets — or whether they should be required to be neutral on the matter. For example, in some cases I.S.P.'s have restricted the routing of services provided by competitors like Internet phone calls.

He answered questions earlier this month by telephone from Cambridge, Mass.

Q. *Why did you decide to speak out on Net neutrality?*

A. I have had an opinion on Net neutrality since I mentioned it in a book — effectively, but not by that name — a long time ago. It's not a new opinion and it's one thing that is shared by such a huge majority, if you like an unwritten assumption of the entire Internet culture. Someone actually thought to challenge it.

Q. *Do you think you would be able to invent the Web today, given the barriers that are emerging?*

C.J. GUNTHER FOR THE NEW YORK TIMES

Sir Tim Berners-Lee, the inventor of the World Wide Web, advocates "Net neutrality," or limiting Internet service providers' control over information.

A. You have to imagine the Net without the Web. I think I would be able to invent it today, but if we lose Net neutrality, then imagine a world in which it's much more difficult to invent the Web.

Q. *Is your view that the anti-Net neutrality infrastructure actually threatens political democracy? Does it go beyond just the technical structure of the Internet?*

A. Net neutrality is one of those principles, social principles, certainly now much more than a technical principle, which is very fundamental. When you break it, then it really depends how far you let things go. But certainly I think that the neutrality of the Net is a medium essential for democracy, yes — if there is democracy and the way people inform themselves is to go onto the Web.

Q. *So there are political consequences. Are there are also economic consequences? If so, what are they?*

A. I think the people who talk about dismantling — threatening — Net neutrality don't appreciate how important it has been for us to have an independent market for productivity and for applications on the Internet.

Now, if we compare what you can get into your home with earliest modems, it's maybe 1,000 times as fast. So that market has been very competitive, very successful.

And I think we wouldn't have seen this explosion in the exciting, tremendous diversity of the kind of things you see on the Web now. So in the future, obviously, we expect to see many more things. We expect to see, very importantly, television streaming over the Internet, which is going to make a very exciting market in television content and maybe entertainment, maybe educational ideas.

The people deploying these things rely on the fact that the Internet is sitting there waiting to carry whatever they can dream up.

Q. *You wrote, at one point, that in the beginning, the data packets weren't inspected. Now I see that many modern routers do packet inspection as a matter of course. Does this make it too late? Is packet inspection by itself a threat to Net neutrality?*

A. No, I think there's been some muddying the waters. Of course, if you're carrying high-resolution video, then you have to treat those packets, for example, differently from packets for chat sessions.

So routers have to be smarter, and they are, to provide this very high functionality that we're asking of them now. Sometimes this involves looking inside the packet. And unfortunately we're also getting to the point where routers have to be able to protect themselves against malicious denial-of-service attacks and so on.

Meanwhile, the government is asking people to put snooping apparatus in routers, so there are all kinds of reasons why routers are starting to become smarter.

That is not an excuse for changing the terms of service of the Internet. The fundamental thing about the Internet is that I connect to the Internet with a certain quality of service — whether it is video- or audio-capable or whatever. If you've connected with the same form of service, then you and I can connect at that level. So if we have both paid for bidirectional, high-definition television, then you and I will also be able to exchange television broadcasts across the Internet. We shouldn't have to negotiate. So the fundamental thing we're talking about here is the deal between the user of the Internet and their Internet service provider.

Q. *You've spoken about the concept of a Dark Net, which would balkanize the Internet. Do you have a nightmare scenario?*

A. In the long term, I'm optimistic because I think even if the United States ends up faltering in its quest for Net neutrality, I think the rest of the world will be horrified, and there will be very strong pressure from other countries who will become a world separate from the U.S., where the Net is neutral. If things go wrong in the States, then I think the result could be that the United States would then have a less-competitive market where content providers could provide a limited selection of all the same old movies to their customers because they have a captive market.

Meanwhile, in other countries, you'd get a much more dynamic and much more competitive market for television over the Internet. So that you'd end up finding that the U.S. would then fall behind and become less competitive until they saw what was going on and fixed it. I just hope we don't have to go through a dark period, a little dark ages while people experiment with dropping Net neutrality and then, perhaps, put it back.

Q. *There are a couple of intriguing technologies on the horizon, and I've wondered whether they will play a positive role in this debate. One is new wireless broadband technologies, which may compete for the*

Internet-to-the-home market. The power line is also a potential avenue of the Internet into the consumer marketplace.

A. I think anything that opens up the competition is clearly going to affect the systems that are more closed. I don't know personally how much hope to put into things like power lines. And in a way, the Internet architecture does cry out against any form of restriction to it because it would just weaken it. And so it could be O.K. if there's an alternative way of getting the bits.

Q. *Do you have a view about the behavior of the telephone companies in this debate? Is this simply traditional monopolist behavior, or is it more subtle? Have you talked to them to understand their motivations?*

A. I have tried, when I've had the opportunity to find out, to understand their motivations, but I can't speak for them. So all I can do is guess. But my guess is that it's not that this is a nefarious planned plot to take over the Internet by a bunch of people who hate it. What I imagine is that it is simply the culture of companies, which have been using a particular business model for a very long time. So I think there is a clash of corporate cultures.

Q. *What do you make of justifications involving quality of service, which would give certain types of Internet data, like voice and video, right of way over other kinds of data?*

A. They say, "It will cost us an awful lot of money for this quality of service, and therefore we will have to disband neutrality." They're not actually logical. Some people say perhaps we ought to be able to charge more for this very special high-bandwidth connectivity. Of course that's fine, charge more. Nobody is suggesting that you shouldn't be able to charge more for a video-capable Internet connection. That's no reason not to make it anything but neutral.

Congress to Take Up Net's Future

BY STEPHEN LABATON | JAN. 10, 2007

WASHINGTON, JAN. 9 — Senior lawmakers, emboldened by the recent restrictions on AT&T and the change in control of Congress, have begun drafting legislation that would prevent high-speed Internet companies from charging content providers for priority access.

The first significant so-called net neutrality legislation of the new Congressional session was introduced Tuesday by Senator Byron L. Dorgan, Democrat of South Dakota, and Senator Olympia J. Snowe of Maine, one of the few Republicans in Congress to support such a measure.

"The success of the Internet has been its openness and the ability of anyone anywhere in this country to go on the Internet and reach the world," Mr. Dorgan said. "If the big interests who control the pipes become gatekeepers who erect tolls, it will have a significant impact on the Internet as we know it."

In the House, Representative Edward J. Markey, the Massachusetts Democrat who heads the Energy and Commerce Subcommittee on Telecommunications and the Internet, said recently that he would introduce legislation soon and planned to hold hearings.

Despite the flurry of activity, the proposals face significant political impediments and no one expects that they will be adopted quickly. But the fight promises to be a bonanza for lobbyists and a fund-raising tool for lawmakers. It pits Internet giants like Google, Yahoo, eBay and Amazon, which support the legislation, against telecommunication titans like Verizon, AT&T and large cable companies like Comcast.

The debate may also affect the plans of the companies to develop new services and to consider certain mergers or acquisitions.

Consumer groups have allied themselves with content providers. The groups maintain that without the legislation, some content providers would be discouraged from offering services while others would impose costs on providers that would either discourage them from offering new services or pass them on to consumers. They also feel that small companies would be unable to compete.

But the telephone and cable companies say that efforts to limit their ability to charge for faster service would discourage the pipeline companies from making billions of dollars in investments to upgrade their networks, and would, as a practical matter, be even more harmful to consumers.

Beyond the debate, the fight over net neutrality is, like most regulatory political battles, a fight over money and competing business models. Companies like Google, Yahoo and many content providers do not want to pay for the kinds of faster Internet service that will enable consumers to more quickly download videos and play games.

In their thirst to continue to grow rapidly, content providers are looking to expand, but they consider any attempt by the telephone and cable companies to charge them for priority services as restricting their ability to move into new areas.

On the other hand, the telephone and cable companies — the so-called Internet pipes — want to be able to charge for access, particularly as they begin competing with content providers by offering their video services and programming.

The phone companies have also been studying a business model not unlike that of the cable TV industry: charging premiums to certain content providers for greater access to their pipes.

They say that existing rules, as well as sound business judgment, would preclude them from trying to degrade or slow their broadband service and that what they oppose is regulation that would prevent them from charging for offering a faster service. They also point out that many content providers are already charging customers for priority services, so that what they are proposing is not unduly restrictive.

While the debate has broken largely along partisan lines — with Democrats among the staunchest supporters and Republicans the biggest foes — there remains considerable Democratic opposition. Last June, a vote on an amendment by Mr. Markey similar to what he plans to introduce failed by 269 to 152, with 58 Democrats voting against the measure.

Many of those Democrats have been allied with unions, which have sided with the phone companies because they believe that the lack of restrictions will encourage the companies to invest and expand their networks.

In the Senate, where the party in the minority has considerably more power than in the House, the measure suffers from similar political problems. Last year the Republicans blocked the measure from reaching the Senate floor.

But several developments have given some momentum to the supporters of the measures. The House is now under the control of the Democrats, and the new speaker, Nancy Pelosi of California, has been a vigorous supporter of the legislation. Ms. Pelosi's district in San Francisco is near Silicon Valley, the home of many companies that have sought the legislation.

Moreover, the conditions that the Federal Communications Commission imposed on AT&T as a condition of its acquisition of SBC Communications represented an important political victory for proponents of the legislation. After one of the five members of the commission removed himself from the proceeding, the commission's two Democrats forced the companies to agree to a two-year moratorium on offering any service that "privileges, degrades or prioritizes any packet" transmitted over its broadband service.

The conditions imposed no significant immediate costs on AT&T. The company does not yet have the equipment in place on its network to offer a priority service on a large scale. But the conditions imposed by the F.C.C. showed that, contrary to assertions of the phone companies, it was possible to draft language that would preclude the companies from discriminating against providers.

The conditions also set a political benchmark of sorts, and gave the supporters of the legislation two years to try to gain more momentum just as all of the companies are trying to figure out their next major sources of revenue.

Verizon Blocks Messages of Abortion Rights Group

BY ADAM LIPTAK | SEPT. 27, 2007

SAYING IT HAD THE RIGHT to block "controversial or unsavory" text messages, Verizon Wireless has rejected a request from Naral Pro-Choice America, the abortion rights group, to make Verizon's mobile network available for a text-message program.

The other leading wireless carriers have accepted the program, which allows people to sign up for text messages from Naral by sending a message to a five-digit number known as a short code.

Text messaging is a growing political tool in the United States and a dominant one abroad, and such sign-up programs are used by many political candidates and advocacy groups to send updates to supporters.

But legal experts said private companies like Verizon probably have the legal right to decide which messages to carry. The laws that forbid common carriers from interfering with voice transmissions on ordinary phone lines do not apply to text messages.

The dispute over the Naral messages is a skirmish in the larger battle over the question of "net neutrality" — whether carriers or Internet service providers should have a voice in the content they provide to customers.

"This is right at the heart of the problem," said Susan Crawford, a visiting professor at the University of Michigan law school, referring to the treatment of text messages. "The fact that wireless companies can choose to discriminate is very troubling."

In turning down the program, Verizon, one of the nation's two largest wireless carriers, told Naral that it does not accept programs from any group "that seeks to promote an agenda or distribute content that, in its discretion, may be seen as controversial or unsavory to any of our users." Naral provided copies of its communications with Verizon to The New York Times.

Nancy Keenan, Naral's president, said Verizon's decision interfered with political speech and activism.

"No company should be allowed to censor the message we want to send to people who have asked us to send it to them," Ms. Keenan said. "Regardless of people's political views, Verizon customers should decide what action to take on their phones. Why does Verizon get to make that choice for them?"

A spokesman for Verizon said the decision turned on the subject matter of the messages and not on Naral's position on abortion. "Our internal policy is in fact neutral on the position," said the spokesman, Jeffrey Nelson. "It is the topic itself" — abortion — "that has been on our list."

Mr. Nelson suggested that Verizon may be rethinking its position. "As text messaging and multimedia services become more and more mainstream," he said, "we are continuing to review our content standards." The review will be made, he said, "with an eye toward making more information available across ideological and political views."

Naral provided an example of a recent text message that it has sent to supporters: "End Bush's global gag rule against birth control for world's poorest women! Call Congress. (202) 224-3121. Thnx! Naral Text4Choice."

Messages urging political action are generally thought to be at the heart of what the First Amendment protects. But the First Amendment limits government power, not that of private companies like Verizon.

In rejecting the Naral program, Verizon appeared to be acting against its economic interests. It would have received a small fee to set up the program and additional fees for messages sent and received.

Text messaging programs based on five- and six-digit short codes are a popular way to receive updates on news, sports, weather and entertainment. Several of the leading Democratic presidential candidates have used them, as have the Republican National Committee, Save Darfur and Amnesty International.

Most of the candidates and advocacy groups that use text message programs are liberal, which may reflect the demographics of the technology's users and developers. A spokeswoman for the National Right to Life Committee, which is in some ways Naral's anti-abortion counterpart, said, for instance, that it has not dabbled in text messaging.

Texting has proved to be an extraordinarily effective political tool. According to a study released this month by researchers at Princeton and the University of Michigan, young people who received text messages reminding them to vote in November 2006 were more likely to go to the polls. The cost per vote generated, the study said, was much smaller than other sorts of get-out-the-vote efforts.

Around the world, the phenomenon is even bigger.

"Even as dramatic as the adoption of text messaging for political communication has been in the United States, we've been quite slow compared to the rest of the world," said James E. Katz, the director of the Center for Mobile Communication Studies at Rutgers University. "It's important in political campaigns and political protests, and it has affected the outcomes of elections."

Timothy Wu, a law professor at Columbia, said it was possible to find analogies to Verizon's decision abroad. "Another entity that controls mass text messages is the Chinese government," Professor Wu said.

Jed Alpert, the chief executive officer of Mobile Commons, which says it is the largest provider of mobile services to political and advocacy groups, including Naral, said he had never seen a decision like Verizon's.

"This is something we haven't encountered before, that is very surprising and that we're concerned about," Mr. Alpert said.

Professor Wu pointed to a historical analogy. In the 19th century, he said, Western Union, the telegraph company, engaged in discrimination, based on the political views of people who sought to send telegrams. "One of the eventual reactions was the common carrier rule," Professor Wu said, which required telegraph and then phone companies to accept communications from all speakers on all topics.

Some scholars said such a rule was not needed for text messages because market competition was sufficient to ensure robust political debate.

"Instead of having the government get in the game of regulating who can carry what, I would get in the game of promoting as many options as possible," said Christopher S. Yoo, a law professor at the University of Pennsylvania. "You might find text-messaging companies competing on their openness policies."

F.C.C. Vote Sets Precedent on Unfettered Web Usage

BY SAUL HANSELL | AUG. 2, 2008

THE FEDERAL COMMUNICATIONS COMMISSION formally voted Friday to uphold the complaint against Comcast, the nation's largest cable company, saying that it had illegally inhibited users of its high-speed Internet service from using popular file-sharing software. The decision, which imposes no fine, requires Comcast to end such blocking this year.

Kevin J. Martin, the commission's chairman, said the order was meant to set a precedent that Internet providers, and indeed all communications companies, could not keep customers from using their networks the way they see fit unless there is a good reason.

"We are preserving the open character of the Internet," Mr. Martin said in an interview after the 3-to-2 vote. "We are saying that network operators can't block people from getting access to any content and any applications."

The case also highlights the broader issue of whether new legislation is needed to force Internet providers to treat all uses of their networks equally, a concept called network neutrality. Some have urged legislation to make sure that big Internet companies do not discriminate against small companies or those that compete with their video or telephone services.

The legal complaint against Comcast, which is based in Philadelphia, relates to BitTorrent, software that is commonly used by people downloading movies, television shows, music and software. Many, but hardly all, of those files are copyrighted material traded without authorization.

Comcast says that a small percentage of its customers using BitTorrent consume a large share of its network capacity, degrading the Internet access of other customers. So it installed equipment that slowed — but did not completely block — file transfers using BitTorrent.

Comcast has already said that it plans to move to a new way of managing its network at times of peak use to avoid singling out certain programs. Nevertheless, the company objected rather strongly to the commission's decision.

"We believe that our network management choices were reasonable, wholly consistent with industry practices," Sena Fitzmaurice, a spokeswoman for the company, said in a statement. "We are considering all our legal options and are disappointed that the commission rejected our attempts to settle this issue without further delays."

Analysts said they expected Comcast to appeal the decision.

The company's blocking received wide publicity last October after The Associated Press ran tests of Comcast's network that substantiated some users' allegations. Two public advocacy groups, Free Press and Public Knowledge, then filed a formal complaint with the commission, which held several hearings into the matter.

Mr. Martin, a Republican, was supported in Friday's decision by the two Democratic commissioners, Jonathan S. Adelstein and Michael J. Copps. The move was opposed by the two other Republican members, Robert M. McDowell and Deborah Taylor Tate.

In a lengthy dissent, Mr. McDowell wrote that the commission did not have the legal authority to take such action because it had never issued formal regulations on the issues in question.

"This matter would have had a better chance on appeal if we had put the horse before the cart and conducted a rule-making, issued rules and then enforced them," he wrote.

Mr. Martin responded that it was common practice for agencies to address new policy issues when dealing with complaints.

Mr. McDowell also wrote that Comcast's systems were a legitimate method of managing the capacity of the network and not an attempt to disadvantage rivals.

"Americans download more than 11 billion Internet videos per month, yet the record contains no evidence that Comcast is interfering with sites like YouTube," he wrote, adding that YouTube does not use the BitTorrent software that was blocked.

Curiously, representatives from other telecommunications companies praised the decision, even though they objected to the commission meddling in how they manage their networks. They said they would prefer such rulings to legislation from Congress, which has discussed enshrining net neutrality principles in the law.

Jim Cicconi, senior executive vice president for external and legislative affairs for AT&T, said in a statement, "Regardless of how one views the merits of the complaint against Comcast, the F.C.C. today has shown that its national Internet policies work, and that they are more than sufficient for handling any net neutrality concerns that may arise."

Edward J. Markey, the Massachusetts Democrat who is chairman of the House Subcommittee on Telecommunications and the Internet, has introduced legislation to mandate network neutrality. He said in a statement that the F.C.C.'s action in fact proved that Congress must act on the issue.

"Vigilance by regulators and policy makers, coupled with a commitment to act when necessary, is vital to thwart the emergence of new bottlenecks to competition and innovation," he said.

CHAPTER 2

Obama's Promise of a Democratic Web

While the earliest debates over net neutrality occurred during the Bush years, it was President Barack Obama who first made net neutrality a campaign promise and drove forward a pro–net neutrality agenda. This process began under the tenure of F.C.C. chair Julius Genachowski, who directed the agency from 2009 to 2013. As Genachowski pushed for a set of net neutrality rules that would protect the public's right to access all legal content online at equal speeds, Republicans in Congress and telecom companies pushed back with their own agenda.

Mr. Obama's Internet Agenda

OPINION | BY THE NEW YORK TIMES | DEC. 15, 2008

PRESIDENT-ELECT BARACK OBAMA recently announced an ambitious plan to build up the nation's Internet infrastructure as part of his proposed economic stimulus package. Upgrading the Internet is a particularly smart kind of stimulus, one that would spread knowledge, promote entrepreneurship and make this country more competitive globally.

The United States has long been the world leader in technology, but when it comes to the Internet, it is fast falling behind. America now ranks 15th in the world in access to high-speed Internet connections. A cornerstone of Mr. Obama's agenda is promoting universal, affordable high-speed Internet.

Mr. Obama, who had notable success with online fund-raising and voter turnout, spoke during the presidential campaign about the transformative power of the Internet to improve Americans' quality of life. He argued that it could, among other things, reduce health care costs, create jobs and make it easier for citizens to participate in government decision-making.

In a speech this month about his economic stimulus plan, he said that he intends to ensure that every child has a chance to get online and that he would use some of the stimulus money to connect libraries and schools. It is a critical goal. Children trapped on the wrong side of the digital divide are deprived of a fair chance to educate themselves and to compete for high-skill, high-paying jobs.

Mr. Obama has also been a strong supporter of "network neutrality," the principle that Internet service providers should not be able to discriminate against any of the information that they carry. Net neutrality laws are necessary to ensure that Internet service providers do not block content they disagree with or give financial breaks to big tech companies, squeezing out smaller competitors and stifling innovation.

Mr. Obama will need to work with Congress — and fight against corporate lobbyists — to accomplish some of his goals. Some he can achieve on his own. With the right appointments to the Federal Communications Commission, he should be able to get good net neutrality regulations.

"This is the Eisenhower Interstate highway moment for the Internet," argues Ben Scott, policy director of the media reform group Free Press. Restoring America to its role as the world's Internet leader could be an important part of Mr. Obama's presidential legacy.

F.C.C. Seeks to Protect Free Flow of Internet Data

BY SAUL HANSELL | SEPT. 18, 2009

IN A MOVE to make good on one of President Obama's campaign promises, Julius Genachowski, the chairman of the Federal Communications Commission, will propose Monday that the agency expand and formalize rules meant to keep Internet providers from discriminating against certain content flowing over their networks, according to several officials briefed on his plans.

In 2005, the commission adopted four broad principles relating to the idea of network neutrality as part of a move to deregulate the Internet services provided by telephone companies. Those principles declared that consumers had the right to use the content, applications, services and devices of their choice using the Internet. They also promoted competition between Internet providers.

In a speech Monday at the Brookings Institution, Mr. Genachowski is expected to outline a proposal to add a fifth principle that will prevent Internet providers from discriminating against certain services or applications. Consumer advocates are concerned that Internet providers might ban or degrade services that compete with their own offerings, like television shows delivered over the Web.

He is also expected to propose that the rules explicitly apply to any Internet service, even if delivered over wireless networks — something that has been unclear until now.

A commission spokeswoman declined to discuss Mr. Genachowski's speech.

Perhaps most significantly, Mr. Genachowski will propose that the net neutrality principles be formally adopted as commission rules, a lengthy procedure that involves several rounds of public comment. His predecessor, Kevin Martin, avoided making formal rules, arguing that the industry changes too quickly. He preferred to respond to complaints when they were filed.

The commission relied on its net neutrality principles when it sanctioned Comcast last year for impeding the Internet connections of some customers who were using certain file-sharing software. The cable company has appealed that ruling, challenging the principles as invalid because the commission adopted them without a formal rule-making process.

Other cable and phone companies have distanced themselves from Comcast's actions. They argue that vague guidelines are preferable to formal rules. Some lobbyists see Mr. Genachowski's move in part as a way to prevent a court from diminishing the commission's powers as a result of Comcast's suit.

Since Mr. Genachowski was one of the main authors of the net neutrality provisions of President Obama's platform, industry watchers thought it was only a matter of time before he would tackle the subject.

While the communications industry does not like more regulation, it has generally not found it difficult to comply with the existing four principles, lobbyists said. But there are a few areas where opposition is expected.

One is over the opportunity some Internet providers see in offering faster or more reliable connections to some companies offering services over the Web. A company offering high-definition movies, for example, might pay an Internet provider to deliver them more quickly.

Some public advocates are concerned that such services might quickly transform the largely egalitarian Internet into a system that offered first-class service only to the wealthiest players, relegating independent sites to the slow lane.

Mr. Genachowski is expected to propose a compromise that would allow some experimentation with premium services but with limits to ensure that sites that do not pay for preferred treatment would continue to be available as they are now.

Another controversial aspect is Mr. Genachowski's assertion that as wireless Internet service becomes faster and more flexible, it should be subject to the same network neutrality rules as wired service.

"We are concerned about the unintended consequences that net neutrality regulation would have on investments from the very industry that's helping to drive the U.S. economy," said the CTIA, the wireless trade group, in a statement.

The commission chairman is expected to propose exceptions that take into account that older generations of cellphones have technical limitations that may keep them from being as open as more modern devices.

Network operators also argue that they should be able to electronically comb through traffic in order to weed out viruses and other malicious activity. The proposal will allow Internet providers to engage in "reasonable network management."

The chairman is expected to ask the commission to start the rule-making process at a meeting in October. After several rounds of comments and responses, a plan could be ready for a final vote by next spring.

Search, but You May Not Find

OPINION | BY ADAM RAFF | DEC. 27, 2009

AS WE BECOME increasingly dependent on the Internet, we need to be increasingly concerned about how it is regulated. The Federal Communications Commission has proposed "network neutrality" rules, which would prohibit Internet service providers from discriminating against or charging premiums for certain services or applications on the Web. The commission is correct that ensuring equal access to the infrastructure of the Internet is vital, but it errs in directing its regulations only at service providers like AT&T and Comcast.

Today, search engines like Google, Yahoo and Microsoft's new Bing have become the Internet's gatekeepers, and the crucial role they play in directing users to Web sites means they are now as essential a component of its infrastructure as the physical network itself. The F.C.C. needs to look beyond network neutrality and include "search neutrality": the principle that search engines should have no editorial policies other than that their results be comprehensive, impartial and based solely on relevance.

The need for search neutrality is particularly pressing because so much market power lies in the hands of one company: Google. With 71 percent of the United States search market (and 90 percent in Britain), Google's dominance of both search and search advertising gives it overwhelming control. Google's revenues exceeded $21 billion last year, but this pales next to the hundreds of billions of dollars of other companies' revenues that Google controls indirectly through its search results and sponsored links.

One way that Google exploits this control is by imposing covert "penalties" that can strike legitimate and useful Web sites, removing them entirely from its search results or placing them so far down the rankings that they will in all likelihood never be found. For three years, my company's vertical search and price-comparison site, Foundem, was effectively “disappeared” from the Internet in this way.

Another way that Google exploits its control is through preferential placement. With the introduction in 2007 of what it calls “universal search,” Google began promoting its own services at or near the top of its search results, bypassing the algorithms it uses to rank the services of others. Google now favors its own price-comparison results for product queries, its own map results for geographic queries, its own news results for topical queries, and its own YouTube results for video queries. And Google’s stated plans for universal search make it clear that this is only the beginning.

Because of its domination of the global search market and ability to penalize competitors while placing its own services at the top of its search results, Google has a virtually unassailable competitive advantage. And Google can deploy this advantage well beyond the confines of search to any service it chooses. Wherever it does so, incumbents are toppled, new entrants are suppressed and innovation is imperiled.

Google’s treatment of Foundem stifled our growth and constrained the development of our innovative search technology. The preferential placement of Google Maps helped it unseat MapQuest from its position as America’s leading online mapping service virtually overnight. The share price of TomTom, a maker of navigation systems, has fallen by some 40 percent in the weeks since the announcement of Google’s free turn-by-turn satellite navigation service. And RightMove, Britain’s leading real-estate portal, lost 10 percent of its market value this month on the mere rumor that Google planned a real-estate search service here.

Without search neutrality rules to constrain Google’s competitive advantage, we may be heading toward a bleakly uniform world of Google Everything — Google Travel, Google Finance, Google Insurance, Google Real Estate, Google Telecoms and, of course, Google Books.

Some will argue that Google is itself so innovative that we needn’t worry. But the company isn’t as innovative as it is regularly given credit for. Google Maps, Google Earth, Google Groups, Google Docs, Google Analytics, Android and many other Google products are all based on technology that Google has acquired rather than invented.

Even AdWords and AdSense, the phenomenally efficient economic engines behind Google's meteoric success, are essentially borrowed inventions: Google acquired AdSense by purchasing Applied Semantics in 2003; and AdWords, though developed by Google, is used under license from its inventors, Overture.

Google was quick to recognize the threat to openness and innovation posed by the market power of Internet service providers, and has long been a leading proponent of net neutrality. But it now faces a difficult choice. Will it embrace search neutrality as the logical extension to net neutrality that truly protects equal access to the Internet? Or will it try to argue that discriminatory market power is somehow dangerous in the hands of a cable or telecommunications company but harmless in the hands of an overwhelmingly dominant search engine?

The F.C.C. is now inviting public comment on its proposed network neutrality rules, so there is still time to persuade the commission to expand the scope of the regulations. In particular, it should ensure that the principles of transparency and nondiscrimination apply to search engines as well as to service providers. The alternative is an Internet in which innovation can be squashed at will by an all-powerful search engine.

ADAM RAFF IS A CO-FOUNDER OF FOUNDEM, AN INTERNET TECHNOLOGY FIRM.

U.S. Court Curbs F.C.C. Authority on Web Traffic

BY EDWARD WYATT | APRIL 6, 2010

WASHINGTON — A federal appeals court ruled on Tuesday that regulators had limited power over Web traffic under current law. The decision will allow Internet service companies to block or slow specific sites and charge video sites like YouTube to deliver their content faster to users.

The court decision was a setback to efforts by the Federal Communications Commission to require companies to give Web users equal access to all content, even if some of that content is clogging the network.

The court ruling, which came after Comcast asserted that it had the right to slow its cable customers' access to a file-sharing service called BitTorrent, could prompt efforts in Congress to change the law in order to give the F.C.C. explicit authority to regulate Internet service.

That could prove difficult politically, however, since some conservative Republicans philosophically oppose giving the agency more power, on the grounds that Internet providers should be able to decide what services they offer and at what price.

More broadly, the ruling by the United States Court of Appeals for the District of Columbia Circuit could raise obstacles to the Obama administration's effort to increase Americans' access to high-speed Internet networks.

For example, the national broadband plan released by the administration last month proposed to shift billions of dollars in money from a fund to provide phone service in rural areas to one that helps pay for Internet access in those areas. Legal observers said the court decision suggested that the F.C.C. did not have the authority to make that switch.

The F.C.C. will now have to reconsider its strategy for mandating "net neutrality," the principle that all Internet content should be treated equally by network providers. One option would be to reclassify broadband service as a sort of basic utility subject to strict regulation, like telephone service. Telephone companies and broadband providers have already indicated that they would vigorously oppose such a move.

The appeals court's 3-0 decision, which was written by one of the court's more liberal members, Judge David S. Tatel, focused on the narrow issue of whether the F.C.C. had authority to regulate Comcast's network management practices.

But it was a clear victory for those who favor limiting the F.C.C.'s regulation of the Internet, said Phil Kerpen, a vice president at Americans for Prosperity, a group that advocates limited government. "The F.C.C. has no legal basis for imposing its dystopian regulatory vision under the net neutrality banner," he said.

As a practical matter, the court ruling will not have any immediate impact on Internet users, since Comcast and other large Internet providers are not currently restricting specific types of Web content and have no plans to do so.

Comcast, the nation's largest cable provider, had a muted reaction to its victory. The company said it was gratified by the court's decision but added that it had changed the management policies that led it to restrict access to BitTorrent, a service used to exchange a range of large data files, from pirated movies to complex software programs.

"Comcast remains committed to the F.C.C.'s existing open Internet principles, and we will continue to work constructively with this F.C.C. as it determines how best to increase broadband adoption and preserve an open and vibrant Internet," Comcast said in a statement.

The company is currently seeking federal approval for its proposed acquisition of a majority stake in NBC Universal, the parent of the NBC broadcast network and a cadre of popular cable channels. Some members of Congress and consumer groups have opposed the merger, saying that it would enable Comcast to favor its own cable channels and discriminate against those owned by competitors — something the company has said it does not intend to do.

After the ruling on Tuesday, consumer advocates voiced similar concerns about Comcast's potential power over the Internet, saying that the company could, for example, give priority to transmission of video services of NBC channels and restrict those owned by a competitor like CBS.

"Internet users now have no cop on the beat," said Ben Scott, policy director for Free Press, a nonprofit organization that supported the F.C.C. in the case.

Julius Genachowski, the chairman of the F.C.C., had said previously that if the agency lost the Comcast case, he would seek to find other legal authority to implement consumer protections over Internet service. In a statement, the F.C.C. said it remained "firmly committed to promoting an open Internet."

While the court decision invalidated its current approach to that goal, the agency said, "the court in no way disagreed with the importance of providing a free and open Internet, nor did it close the door to other methods for achieving this important end."

The concept of equal access for all Internet content is one that people who favor some degree of F.C.C. regulation say is necessary not only to protect consumers but also to foster innovation and investment in technology.

"You can't have innovation if all the big companies get the fast lane," said Gigi B. Sohn, president of Public Knowledge, which advocates for consumer rights on digital issues. "Look at Google, eBay, Yahoo — none of those companies would have survived if 15 years ago we had a fast lane and a slow lane on the Internet."

The court's ruling could potentially affect content providers like Google, which owns YouTube, a popular video-sharing service. Content providers fear that Internet service companies will ask them to pay a fee to ensure delivery of material like high-definition video that takes up a lot of network capacity.

Google declined to comment directly on the ruling but pointed to the Open Internet Coalition, of which it is a member. The coalition's executive director, Markham Erickson, said the decision "creates a dangerous situation, one where the health and openness of the Internet is being held hostage by the behavior of the major telco and cable providers."

Sam Feder, a lawyer who formerly served as general counsel for the F.C.C., said that the court's decision "is the worst of all worlds for the F.C.C." He said the opinion was written narrowly enough that it was unlikely to be successfully appealed, while also raising enough possibilities of other ways that the F.C.C. could accomplish the same goals that it was unlikely to inspire Congressional action to give the agency specific regulatory authority over the Internet.

Under the Bush administration, the F.C.C. largely deregulated Internet service. But in 2008, the final year of the administration, the agency decided to impose the net neutrality order on Comcast. Under President Obama, the F.C.C. has broadened that initiative, seeking to craft rules governing the entire industry.

Tuesday's ruling was the latest in a string of court decisions that rebuffed efforts by the F.C.C. to expand its regulatory authority, noted Eli M. Noam, a professor of finance and economics at the Columbia University graduate business school and the director of the Columbia Institute for Tele-Information.

"The F.C.C. is going to have to be more careful in how it proceeds," he said, suggesting that the agency would have to structure policy decisions that were more broadly acceptable to the major telecommunications industry players in order to give them some legitimacy.

Andrew M. Odlyzko, a professor at the University of Minnesota who has served as director of the university's Digital Technology Center, said that while some service providers might jump at the opportunity to establish toll roads for broadband, the biggest companies, including Comcast and Verizon, have said they do not intend to do so.

F.C.C. Proposes Rules on Internet Access

BY EDWARD WYATT | MAY 6, 2010

WASHINGTON — The chairman of the Federal Communications Commission outlined a plan on Thursday that would allow the agency to control the transmission component of high-speed Internet, but not rates or content.

In announcing the F.C.C. decision, Julius Genachowski, the commission's chairman, said the agency would begin a process to reclassify broadband transmission service as a telecommunications service, subjecting the Internet to some of the same oversight as telephone services.

But, he said, the commission would also exempt broadband service from many of the rules affecting telephone service, seeking mainly to guarantee that Internet service providers could not discriminate against certain applications, Internet sites or users.

The approach would specifically forbid the commission from regulating rates charged by telephone and cable companies for Internet service and would not allow the commission to regulate Internet content, services, applications or electronic commerce sites.

The approach, Mr. Genachowski said, maintains the "status quo" and is intended to be "consistent with the longstanding consensus regarding the limited but essential role that the government should play with respect to broadband communications."

Opponents, including some telecommunications companies that provide broadband Internet service, said the approach would create uncertainty and legal battles that would slow the development of technologies that could benefit consumers.

They also said that in making the legal justification for its decision, the commission seemed to be arguing the opposite of what it had previously asserted in a Supreme Court case on Internet regulation.

The new regulatory framework was made necessary, Mr. Genachowski said, by a federal appeals court decision last month involving Comcast, the nation's largest cable company, that invalidated the approach that the F.C.C. had taken to regulating broadband service.

Under that approach, the commission maintained that it had "ancillary authority" to oversee certain aspects of broadband service even though it did not fall under the strict rules that give the commission the power to regulate telephone service.

The United States Court of Appeals for the District of Columbia Circuit said in April that the F.C.C.'s classification of broadband service as an "information service" rather than as a "telecommunications service" did not allow it to sanction Comcast for slowing or blocking access by its customers to an application known as BitTorrent, which is used to share large data files including video and audio.

The new approach, which the F.C.C. called a "third way," would rely on a legal theory that recognizes the computing function and the broadband transmission component of retail Internet access service as separate things subject to different regulation.

The approach is similar to one that the commission has used to regulate aspects of wireless communications service, Mr. Genachowski said. And it relies in part on a 2005 United States Supreme Court decision, National Cable and Telecommunications Association v. Brand X Internet Services. In that case, the court said that Congress gave the F.C.C. the authority to decide how it would regulate Internet service.

But the F.C.C.'s new approach also relies in part on a dissenting opinion in that case, written by Justice Antonin Scalia, which said that the "computing functionality" and the broadband transmission component of Internet access service were different things, each subject to differing levels of regulation.

Austin C. Schlick, general counsel for the F.C.C., said in a statement that "the upshot is that the commission is able to tailor the requirements" of its regulatory authority "so that they conform precisely to the policy consensus for broadband transmission services."

Telecommunications companies said they believed the F.C.C. had overstepped. The National Cable and Telecommunications Association, with whom the F.C.C. sided in the Brand X case, called the decision "fraught with legal uncertainty and practical consequences which pose real risks to our ability to provide the high-quality and innovative services that our customers expect."

Thomas J. Tauke, an executive vice president at Verizon, said the new approach was "legally unsupported" and could only bring "confusion and delay to the important work of continuing to build the nation's broadband future."

Part of the uncertainty, opponents said, would result from the possibility that future F.C.C. leaders could decide that they wanted to reverse the decision, just as Mr. Genachowski reversed a previous commission's ruling.

Consumer advocates praised the decision, at least in part. Public Knowledge, a consumer interest group, said it supported the approach but was dismayed by the commission's decision that "open access" provisions of the Communications Act — which require companies to share access to the physical lines of connection that enter consumers' homes — did not apply to broadband access as they did to basic telephone service.

Joel Kelsey, a policy analyst for Consumers Union, said the F.C.C. "appears to have found a way to ensure it has the authority to protect consumers from potential anticompetitive actions by providers of broadband services."

Comcast, which successfully fought the commission over its regulatory authority, said in a statement that it was prepared "to work constructively" with the F.C.C. on "limited but effective measures" to preserve an open Internet, as long as they did not put the industry under a regulatory cloud.

Web Plan From Google and Verizon Is Criticized

BY CLAIRE CAIN MILLER AND MIGUEL HELFT | AUG. 9, 2010

SAN FRANCISCO — Google and Verizon on Monday introduced a proposal for how Internet service should be regulated — and were immediately criticized by groups that favor keeping the network as open as possible.

According to the proposal, Internet service providers would not be able to block producers of online content or offer them a paid "fast lane." It says the Federal Communications Commission should have the authority to stop or fine any rule-breakers.

The proposal, however, carves out exceptions for Internet access over cellphone networks, and for potential new services that broadband providers could offer. In a joint blog post, the companies said these could include things like health care monitoring, "advanced educational services, or new entertainment and gaming options."

The two companies are hoping to influence regulators and lawmakers in the debate over a principle known as net neutrality, which holds that Internet users should have equal access to all types of information online.

This principle is crucial for consumers and for fostering innovation among Internet entrepreneurs, Eric E. Schmidt, Google's chief executive, said in a call with reporters. "The next two people in a garage really do need an open Internet," he said.

But some proponents of net neutrality say that by excluding wireless and other online services, Google and Verizon are creating a loophole that could allow carriers to circumvent regulation meant to ensure openness.

The plan "creates an Internet for the haves and an Internet for the have-nots," said Andrew Jay Schwartzman, senior vice president and policy director at the Media Access Project, an advocacy group in Washington and a member, along with Google, of the Open

Internet Coalition. "It may make some services unaffordable for consumers and access to those services unavailable to new start-ups."

Ivan Seidenberg, chief executive of Verizon, said the proposal excluded cellphone networks because the companies were "concerned about the imposition of too many rules" that could slow the growth of the wireless Web.

The proposal also excludes services that broadband providers may create. These services, the companies said, would have to be "distinguishable from traditional broadband Internet access services and are not designed to circumvent the rules." Mr. Seidenberg said that, for example, the Metropolitan Opera might decide to stream its performances in 3-D through such a service because it would otherwise require too much bandwidth.

Mr. Schmidt said Google had no plans to develop these types of online services.

But some expressed fears that this exception could let companies bypass open-access regulations. For example, an online video start-up could create a competitor to YouTube that did not run on the public Internet and would pay for faster connections to viewers. As those types of payments grew, the access companies might have less incentive to invest in Internet capacity, pushing more content providers to these special services and creating alternative networks that look similar to cable TV.

Jason Hirschhorn, a former president of MySpace and a former executive at MTV Networks, said more questions about the proposal needed to be answered, since the exceptions for new services could be interpreted as "just another way of going against net neutrality."

"Imagine a world where ABC, Comedy Central, MTV, any of these brands, were on some other network, and then there was this open Internet," he said.

Google and Verizon stressed that their plan was not a business deal, but was a policy proposal that both companies intended to follow and that they wanted the Federal Communications Commission to review. The F.C.C., which since June had been convening meetings of Internet companies, carriers and public interest groups to try to come to an agreement on access issues, called off the talks last week after reports that Google and Verizon had come to a private agreement.

One F.C.C. commissioner came out against the proposal. "Some will claim this announcement moves the discussion forward. That's one of its many problems," the commissioner, Michael J. Copps, said in a statement. "It is time to move a decision forward — a decision to reassert F.C.C. authority over broadband telecommunications, to guarantee an open Internet now and forever, and to put the interests of consumers in front of the interests of giant corporations."

Jen Howard, a spokeswoman for the F.C.C., said that it would not immediately comment on the proposal, and that the views of commissioners did not reflect those of Julius Genachowski, the F.C.C. chairman.

Mr. Genachowski said last week that "any deal that doesn't preserve the freedom and openness of the Internet for consumers and entrepreneurs will be unacceptable."

In a speech at the Brookings Institution late last year, Mr. Genachowski addressed the wireless issue, saying that "it is essential that the Internet itself remain open, however users reach it." But he seemed to show some flexibility on other services.

"I also recognize that there may be benefits to innovation and investment of broadband providers offering managed services in limited circumstances," he said, adding that such services "can supplement — but must not supplant — free and open Internet access."

Rebecca Arbogast, a telecommunications analyst at Stifel Nicolaus, predicted that the F.C.C. would probably demand that any net neutrality rules cover wireless, and that the details of any exceptions for specialized online services be made clear.

Silicon Valley companies seemed wary of the proposal. EBay said it would review the suggestions. Paul Misener, vice president for global public policy at Amazon.com, said that although the company agreed that network operators should be able to offer additional services, "we are concerned that this proposal appears to condone services that could harm consumer Internet access."

Groups and companies opposed to open-access regulation also had guarded reactions. AT&T said that it would examine the proposal closely, and that "the Verizon-Google agreement demonstrates that it is possible to bridge differences on this issue."

Gregory L. Rosston, a former deputy chief economist at the Federal Communications Commission and deputy director of the Stanford Institute for Economic Policy Research, said keeping wireless networks free from regulation made sense, because of good competition among wireless providers. "The more competition you have for broadband access, the less need you have for net-neutrality-type regulation," he said.

BRIAN STELTER CONTRIBUTED REPORTING FROM NEW YORK.

Web Plan Is Dividing Companies

BY CLAIRE CAIN MILLER AND BRIAN STELTER | AUG. 11, 2010

IN AN EMERGING BATTLE over regulating Internet access, companies are taking sides.

Facebook, one of the companies that has flourished on the open Internet, indicated Wednesday that it did not support a proposal by Google and Verizon that critics say could let providers of Internet access chip away at that openness.

Meanwhile an executive of AT&T, one of the companies that stands to profit from looser regulations, called the proposal a "reasonable framework."

Most media companies have stayed mute on the subject, but in an interview this week, the media mogul Barry Diller called the proposal a sham.

And outside of technology circles, most people have not yet figured out what is at stake.

The debate revolves around net neutrality, which in the broadest sense holds that Internet users should have equal access to all types of information online, and that companies offering Internet service should not be able to give priority to some sources or types of content.

In a policy statement on Monday, Google and Verizon proposed that regulators enforce those principles on wired connections but not on the wireless Internet. They also excluded something they called "additional, differentiated online services."

In other words, on mobile phones or on special access lanes, carriers like Verizon and AT&T could charge content companies a toll for faster access to customers or, some analysts worry, block certain services from reaching customers altogether.

Opponents of the proposal say that the Internet, suddenly, would not be so open anymore.

"All of our life goes through this network, increasingly, and if you can't reach your boss or get to your remotely stored work, or it's so slow that you can't get it done before you give up and you go to bed, that's a problem," said Allen S. Hammond IV, director of the Broadband Institute of California at Santa Clara University School of Law. "People need to understand that's what we're debating here."

Decisions about net neutrality rest with the Federal Communications Commission and legislators, and full-throated lobbying campaigns are already under way on all sides. The Google-Verizon proposal was essentially an attempt to frame the debate.

It set off a flood of reaction, much of it negative, from Web companies and consumer advocacy groups. In the most extreme situation that opponents envision, two Internets could emerge — the public one known today, and a private one with faster lanes and expensive tolls.

Google and Verizon defended the exemptions by saying that they were giving carriers the flexibility they need to ensure that the Internet's infrastructure remains "a platform for innovation." Carriers say they need to be able to manage their networks as they see fit and generate revenue to expand them.

AT&T said in a statement Wednesday night that "the Verizon-Google agreement demonstrates that it is possible to bridge differences on this issue."

Much of the debate rests on the idea of paid "fast lanes." Content companies, the theory goes, would have to pay for favored access to a carrier's customers, so some Web sites or video services could load faster than others.

That would be a big change from the level playing field that content companies now enjoy, Mr. Diller, who oversees Expedia, Ticketmaster, Match.com and other sites, said last month. Speaking of the telecommunications carriers, he said, "They want the equivalent of having the toaster pay for the ability to plug itself into the electrical grid."

These fast lanes are fairly easy to understand when it comes to wireless Internet access. But what confused many was the suggestion by Google and Verizon that future online services that are not part of the public Internet should also be exempt from equal-access rules.

These services would be "distinguishable from traditional broadband Internet access services," the two companies said in a joint blog post. "It is too soon to predict how these new services will develop, but examples might include health care monitoring, the smart grid, advanced educational services or new entertainment and gaming options."

Some experts were puzzled as to what these services might be and why such an exception might be necessary.

"Broadband that's not the Internet? I don't know what they're talking about," said David A. Patterson, a professor of computer science at the University of California, Berkeley. "They seem to have an idea of something other than the public Internet as a way to ship information, but by nature, to have value it has to go to a lot of places, and right now, that's the packet-switched Internet."

Josh Silver, chief executive of the nonprofit group Free Press, said the exemptions amounted to "the cable-ization of the Internet," in that cable subscribers pay extra for premium tiers of service and for certain channels. Mr. Silver's group is promoting a petition to the F.C.C. titled "Don't Let Google Be Evil." Silicon Valley investors have expressed trepidation that the new rules, if adopted, could put a damper on innovation, particularly for mobile start-ups.

The wireless Internet is quickly emerging as the dominant technology platform, said Matt Cohler, a general partner at Benchmark Capital, a prominent venture firm in Silicon Valley that has invested in start-ups like Twitter. "It is as important to have the right protections in place for the newer platform as it is for the older platform."

Facebook sounded a similar note on Wednesday, saying in a statement that it supported net neutrality principles for both wired and wireless networks.

"Preserving an open Internet that is accessible to innovators — regardless of their size or wealth — will promote a vibrant and competitive marketplace where consumers have ultimate control over the content and services delivered through their Internet connections," the company said.

Technology companies like Amazon and eBay also expressed concern with Google's compromise, but have been less vocal.

Some start-ups see possible advantages in tiered access. Danny Stein, the chairman of eMusic, a music download service, said there needed to be Internet service that remained open and neutral, "but that doesn't mean there can't be premium options to appeal to some amazing consumer experience outside of the garden of net neutrality."

The silence of big media companies like Comcast and the News Corporation on the issue has been noticeable. Media companies' traditional business models have been about controlled pathways to the customer, and they may see benefits in restoring some of that control.

Mr. Diller asserted that the Google-Verizon proposal "doesn't preserve 'net neutrality,' full stop, or anything like it." Asked if other media executives were staying quiet because they stand to gain from a less open Internet, he said simply, "Yes."

MIGUEL HELFT, BROOKS BARNES AND JOSEPH PLAMBECK CONTRIBUTED REPORTING.

Google Plan With Verizon Disillusions Some Allies

BY CLAIRE CAIN MILLER AND MIGUEL HELFT | AUG. 15, 2010

SAN FRANCISCO — On Friday at lunchtime, as Google employees dined al fresco, a hundred protesters descended on the company's Silicon Valley campus. A group called the Raging Grannies sang a song called "The Battle Hymn for the Internet," and others carried signs reading, "Google is evil if the price is right."

They were there to complain about what they saw as Google's about-face on how Internet access should be regulated and to deliver a petition with about 300,000 signatures.

Several of the groups at the protest, like MoveOn.org and Free Press, once saw Google as their top corporate ally in the fight for net neutrality — the principle that the Internet should be a level playing field, with all applications and services treated equally.

But a week ago, Google stunned many of its allies by crossing the aisle and teaming up with Verizon Communications to propose that net neutrality rules should not apply to wireless access and to outline rules for the wired Internet that critics say are riddled with loopholes.

Google's compromise with Verizon is the latest collision between idealism and pragmatism at the company, which has long promoted the idea that its mission, organizing the world's information, is for the public good, as underscored by its unofficial motto: "Don't be evil."

Some say that as Google has grown up and become a large multinational company, it has been forced to start weighing its business interests against the more idealistic leanings of its founders and many of its employees.

"I don't know that Google pondered the moral decision this time," said Jordan Rohan, an Internet and digital media analyst at Stifel Nicolaus. "I think the business decision to cooperate with Verizon superseded the other complications and side effects that it may cause."

JIM WILSON/THE NEW YORK TIMES

Groups protested Google's recent moves that they believe will adversely affect net neutrality.

Google strongly defends its proposal with Verizon, saying it does not violate net neutrality principles and, if adopted by regulators, would protect wired Internet access more than it is protected now.

"We don't view this as a retreat at all," Alan Davidson, Google's director of public policy, said in an interview. "Google believes very strongly in net neutrality."

But the proposal left Google's former allies, as well as many other technology and media companies, feeling disappointed and even betrayed. The risk, they say, is that without adequate regulation, Internet access companies could exercise too much control over what their customers can do online, or how quickly they can gain access to certain content. They could charge companies for faster access to consumers, hurting smaller players and innovation.

"Google has been the most reliable corporate ally to the public interest community," said Josh Silver, president of Free Press, an advocacy group. "That is why their sellout on net neutrality is so stunning."

The proposal from Google and Verizon was all the more surprising to some advocates because it was released just as broader talks brokered by the Federal Communications Commission were close to producing a draft compromise agreement, according to three people briefed on the talks, who agreed to speak on the condition of anonymity because the talks were supposed to be confidential.

Unlike the Google-Verizon proposal, the agreement would have imposed some rules on wireless Internet, these people said.

"We were very close," said one person briefed on the talks. Both the F.C.C. and Google declined to comment on those discussions. After reports of a Google-Verizon deal emerged, the F.C.C. called off the talks, which in addition to those two companies included AT&T, a cable industry group, Skype and the Open Internet Coalition.

Though Google has long said that it thinks openness rules should be applied broadly to Internet access, the company was persuaded that wireless is different because it is evolving rapidly and there is more competition, Mr. Davidson said. Wireless carriers say they need more leeway to manage their networks because it is difficult and expensive for them to add more capacity.

The shift was also a pragmatic compromise to get "broader support, in this case from Verizon and hopefully others," he said.

Still, Google's new position on net neutrality represents a scaling back of the company's ambitious goals. When Google began building a presence in Washington in 2005, net neutrality was one of the first issues it embraced. And over the years, Google's drive to open up the wireless industry became a corporate mission, backed by the company's financial might.

In 2007, Google made a $4.7 billion bid in a government auction of wireless airwaves. The company's goal was not to win the auction, but to raise the price above a threshold that would set off rules forcing openness on the airwaves. Verizon won the auction and soon plans to deploy a high-speed network that will be bound by those rules.

In January, Google introduced its own phone, the Nexus One, and opened an online store to distribute it. By selling directly to consumers, Google was challenging the control that wireless carriers have over the distribution of phones, especially in the United States. But Google quietly killed the Nexus One and the phone store this year.

Analysts say Google's new, more conciliatory approach to the wireless industry was born of necessity.

Verizon offers a number of smartphones that run the Android software from Google, and Verizon is handling growing amounts of data flowing through its network to and from those phones. The volume will only increase as new mobile devices are developed and people use them to watch movies and do other bandwidth-intensive activities. Meanwhile, Google is looking to the mobile Web to feed much of its future growth.

"This is about Google becoming friendlier with the wireless industry so that more Google searches are conducted on wireless devices," Mr. Rohan said. If wireless was exempted from net neutrality rules, Verizon could limit the use of some applications and spend less money improving its network, or get paid by Web companies for delivering content.

Some people see echoes of Google's decision to go into China in 2006. In that case, after a lengthy internal debate, Google put aside its aversion to censorship and decided to enter what quickly became the world's largest Internet market. Google has since pulled its search engine out of mainland China after online attacks that originated there, but the decision to do business there tarnished the company's reputation among human rights advocates and disappointed many employees.

"I don't fault Google and Verizon for striking a deal," said Susan Crawford, a professor at the Benjamin N. Cardozo Law School and a longtime supporter of net neutrality. "A large private company is

JIM WILSON/THE NEW YORK TIMES

A protest at Google in Mountain View, Calif., against a Google-Verizon proposal on Internet access.

always going to operate in its own interest, and for anyone to believe otherwise would be naïve."

Professor Crawford, who is critical of the proposal, said the F.C.C.'s lack of action on access rules pushed Google to seek a compromise. "Google had no choice but to cooperate with the friendliest carrier it can find, which is Verizon," she said.

But disappointed consumers and advocates seem to be holding Google to a different standard, in large part because of the image it created.

"If the world of business is an ugly world full of rats, they've managed to create a bushy tail for themselves and come across as a very, very cute rat with terms like 'Do no evil,'" said Scott Galloway, professor of brand strategy at the Stern School of Business at New York University. "The downside of that is that people have expectations that they're going to fight these quixotic battles, and the bottom line is their obligation to their shareholders."

Not all believe that Google has betrayed its principles. Some longtime Silicon Valley chroniclers say they still think Google is trying to do the right thing, not only for itself, but also for the Internet as a whole.

"I would rather have a company like Google that means to do no evil and is struggling with compromises on these hard issues than a company that doesn't see a struggle," said Tim O'Reilly, founder and chief executive of the technology publisher O'Reilly Media. "Most companies don't even see things in those terms."

ASHLEE VANCE CONTRIBUTED REPORTING FROM MOUNTAIN VIEW, CALIF.

The Struggle for What We Already Have

OPINION | BY JOE NOCERA | SEPT. 3, 2010

FOR SOMETHING that seems so simple and straightforward, "net neutrality" has sure created one big mess.

Net neutrality, of course, is the principle that Internet service providers should not be allowed to favor some Internet content over other content by delivering it faster.

Really, who could be against such a thing? President Obama came out for net neutrality during his presidential campaign. Julius Genachowski, his former law review colleague and basketball buddy, who helped him arrive at that campaign position, is now the chairman of the Federal Communication Commission.

Right-thinking public interest groups, like Public Knowledge ("Fighting for your digital rights in Washington") are fierce, unyielding proponents of net neutrality, viewing its goodness as obvious. Google professes to be a champion of net neutrality. So does Skype. Even the Internet service providers say they favor it.

And yet, here we are, a year and a half into the Obama presidency, and net neutrality is no closer to being encoded in federal regulation than it was when George W. Bush was president. Just this week, the F.C.C. asked for comments on two of the issues surrounding net neutrality, issues that have been hashed over for months. It was an obvious effort to push any decision beyond the midterm elections.

The F.C.C.'s punt doesn't begin to get at the turmoil. When Google and Verizon, a month ago, put together a well-meaning proposal for enforceable net neutrality rules, the two companies were vilified by the net neutrality purists — because they wanted to exempt wireless. "There was universal condemnation of Google for abandoning its 'don't be evil' ethos," said Art Brodsky, the chief spokesman for Public Knowledge — the very group that was leading said condemnation.

In the wake of the Google-Verizon announcement, the F.C.C. abruptly called off talks among the various parties aimed at coming up with net neutrality rules. The talks have since been restarted, more or less, though without the involvement of the F.C.C. Yet even if the talks succeed, the resulting framework wouldn't have the force of law, so it is hard to know precisely what they would accomplish.

And last but not least: thanks to a court decision in March — a decision that resulted directly from the F.C.C.'s effort to punish one big Internet service provider, Comcast, for violating the principle of net neutrality — the agency's very authority to regulate broadband is in doubt.

Surely, this has to rank as the Mother of All Unintended Consequences: there is an outside chance that in its zeal to make net neutrality the law of the land, the F.C.C. could wind up as a regulator with very little to regulate.

Did I mention that this was a big mess?

"Net neutrality arguments have been reduced to bumper stickers," sighed Craig Moffett of Sanford C. Bernstein, Wall Street's premier telecom analyst. Mr. Moffett's point is that like most political slogans that wind up on bumper stickers, the issue isn't nearly as simple and straightforward as it might appear to be at first. Net neutrality is, in fact, incredibly complicated.

Data networks, after all, have to be managed. The engineering is complex. The capacity is limited. Inevitably, some form of prioritization is bound to take place. Rules also have to be created that will give companies the incentive they need to spend the billions upon billions of dollars necessary to extend broadband's reach and improve its speed, so we can catch up to, say, South Korea.

Thus, the public interest view that all data traffic on the Internet should be treated the same is unrealistic. This is especially true with wireless Internet, where the rise of such bandwidth hogs as iPhone apps is starting to outstrip the capacity of the network to transport all the data. (That's one reason the AT&T network, the only carrier for iPhone data, seems so substandard. It is being overwhelmed by all those iPhones.)

The complications notwithstanding, net neutrality, broadly speaking, is what exists now. Among the many benefits net neutrality brings is that it fosters innovation. The great fear of the net neutrality purists, however, is that without federal rules, the Internet providers will begin cutting deals with content providers to give certain traffic priority over other traffic. For instance, Verizon could cut a deal with YouTube that allowed its videos to stream faster than, say, a Hulu video. Or it could even block Hulu. Or it could begin charging consumers extra for Netflix movies that were of better quality than ordinary streaming. As Harold Feld, Public Knowledge's legal director, puts it: "Companies do what companies do."

(Which brings up one of the true oddities about the fervor over net neutrality. Cable television distributors make decisions all the time about what people can see and how much they have to pay for it. If special sports-only tiers aren't an example of placing some content over other content, I don't know what is. Yet because it is merely television, and not the sacred Internet, nobody seems to view this practice as a crime against humanity. But I digress.)

Indeed, what touched off the current furor was the revelation two years ago that one Internet service provider, Comcast, was putting some content over other content. It was slowing down downloads through BitTorrent — a service that, I might add, is used largely to illegally download music and movies. Those BitTorrent downloads, in turn, were slowing down traffic for everybody else. This was Comcast's way of dealing with the problem.

I suspect that anyone who lives with an 18-year-old movie buff would approve of what Comcast did. Nevertheless, the Open Internet Coalition, as the net neutrality purists call themselves, was outraged. So was the F.C.C., which was then led by Kevin Martin, a well-known hater of Comcast. Mr. Martin's F.C.C. took after the company for violating net neutrality principles — principles that were (as they still are) purely voluntary. Comcast sued.

Two years later, by which time Mr. Genachowski had become the chairman of the F.C.C., the court of appeals in Washington ruled that the agency had no grounds for reprimanding Comcast — because, amazingly, it had no authority over broadband under Title I of the 1996 Telecommunications Act, something the agency had long claimed.

This, of course, created a rather large problem. How was it going to impose net neutrality rules — not to mention universal service, public health and safety rules and other regulations related to broadband service — if it had no jurisdiction?

Since that ruling came down in March, the agency has been going down two tracks at the same time. It has been desperately trying to find a way to re-establish jurisdiction over broadband services, while at the same time continuing to push for net neutrality. It has become a very complicated dance.

In May, for instance, Mr. Genachowski proposed that the F.C.C. could use Title II of the Telecommunications Act to re-establish jurisdiction. (Trust me: You don't want to know the details.) But Title II brings with it all sorts of onerous, outmoded regulations better suited to the age of rotary telephones — including price regulation. Although Mr. Genachowski vows not to impose such regulation, who is to say that his successor will agree with his "forbearance" approach (as he calls it)?

And no matter how strenuously Mr. Genachowski vows not to impose price regulations, the Internet service providers have made it plain that they will sue to prevent the F.C.C. from asserting Title II jurisdiction over broadband. It is not inconceivable that the providers will win. At which point, the F.C.C. might as well close up shop. (Did I mention this was a big mess?)

It is this strange stew — uncertainty over jurisdiction, combined with a campaign pledge to establish net neutrality — that explains the recent Google-Verizon proposal. The truth is, virtually every player involved wants the F.C.C. to have oversight over broadband services. Otherwise, chaos is likely to ensue.

Without the F.C.C., the Federal Trade Commission would probably wind up serving as the Internet's sheriff, using antitrust law as its guide and bringing tough enforcement actions. Nobody in the industry wants that.

That's why, at the request of the F.C.C.'s chief of staff, Edward P. Lazarus, representatives from all the sides of the issue, including the Open Internet Coalition, convened to see if they could come up with a framework for net neutrality they could all agree on — and that the F.C.C. could supervise. When those talks bogged down, Google and Verizon decided to come up with their own plan, thinking that they could help lead the others into the light.

Instead, they were slammed. Why? Because even though the framework they came up called for no discrimination of Web sites, for transparency and for all sorts of good things when it came to the kind of broadband that came in through a pipe, it exempted wireless broadband.

Google's rationale — and, without question, Google was the one that compromised — is that wireless was still too new, and the capacity constraints were still too severe, to impose net neutrality, at least at this point. To put it another way, Google was looking at the issue realistically, instead of theologically.

So there we now stand. Net neutrality is in limbo because the public interest purists believe that any compromise is a sellout, and because the F.C.C. so badly shot itself in the foot by pursuing the Comcast case. It is difficult to see how we're ever going to get net neutrality rules.

Then again, maybe the current snarl isn't such a bad thing. "If everybody just walked away, the probability of anything bad happening is quite small," said Mr. Moffett. I agree. Consumers have come to expect an open Internet, and companies will violate net neutrality at their peril. That is just the way the Internet has evolved.

But don't spread that around, O.K.? With so many hours spent on this thing, who really wants to admit that it's much ado about very little?

F.C.C. Approves Net Rules and Braces for Fight

BY BRIAN STELTER | DEC. 21, 2010

WANT TO WATCH hours of YouTube videos or sort through Facebook photos on the computer? Your Internet providers would be forbidden from blocking you under rules approved by the Federal Communications Commission on Tuesday. But if you want to do the same on your cellphone, you may not have the same protections.

The debate over the rules, intended to preserve open access to the Internet, seems to have resulted in a classic Washington solution — the kind that pleases no one on either side of the issue. Verizon and other service providers would prefer no government involvement. Public interest advocates think the rules stop far short of ensuring free speech. Some Republicans believe the rules are another instance of government overreach.

At the commission meeting in Washington, Julius Genachowski, the F.C.C. chairman, said the steps were historic. "For the first time," he said, "we'll have enforceable rules of the road to preserve Internet freedom and openness."

The rules, which address some of the principles of so-called network neutrality, will be tested in the courts in the months ahead, and Republicans said Tuesday that they would challenge the rules in Congress as well.

The new rules are, at best, net semi-neutrality. They ban any outright blocking and any "unreasonable discrimination" of Web sites or applications by fixed-line broadband providers, but they afford more wiggle room to wireless providers like AT&T and Verizon.

They require all providers to disclose what steps they take to manage their networks. In a philosophical break with open Internet advocates, the rules do not explicitly forbid "paid prioritization," which would allow a company to pay for faster transmission of data.

Nonetheless, supporters said the 3-2 vote by the commission

represented significant progress toward fulfilling a campaign promise by President Obama to preserve a level playing field for Web developers. In a statement, Mr. Obama congratulated the F.C.C. and said that the government would "remain vigilant and see to it that innovation is allowed to flourish, that consumers are protected from abuse, and that the democratic spirit of the Internet remains intact."

The rules are set to take effect early in 2011.

The media mogul Barry Diller, chairman of the IAC/InterActive Corporation, said in an interview Tuesday that he thought the F.C.C. had achieved "as much as could be done." The rules of the road, he said, are "going to deter the bad behavior that I think was coming closer and closer."

That "bad behavior" is largely theoretical to date, but as the Internet becomes the pipeline for all the world's text, audio and video, clashes are likely to occur between the owners of the pipe and the people who want to supply innovative services through it.

Mr. Genachowski reiterated on Tuesday that the F.C.C. would "fulfill its historic role as a cop on the beat." But there was considerable disagreement on Tuesday about whether the F.C.C. had the legal authority to go forward with the rules under Title II of the Communications Act.

Hinting that it has doubts about that, Verizon said the F.C.C. order "appears to assert broad authority for sweeping new regulation of broadband wireline and wireless networks and the Internet itself" without "solid statutory underpinnings." In the long term, Verizon said, "that is harmful to consumers and the nation."

Many others sounded more satisfied by Tuesday's decision. Comcast and Time Warner Cable each separately said the F.C.C. had struck a "workable balance," and AT&T said the compromise appeared "to balance major differences."

The fact that the rules received support — even the lukewarm kind — from big businesses should worry consumers, some public interest groups said Tuesday.

"There is a reason that so many giant phone and cable companies are happy, and we are not. These rules are riddled with loopholes,"

Andrew Jay Schwartzman, the policy director for the nonprofit Media Access Project, said in one representative statement. "They foreshadow years of uncertainty and regulatory confusion, which those carriers will use to their advantage."

Other groups warned that the rules would smooth the way for fast and slow lanes on the Internet. They objected especially loudly to the looser rules for wireless devices, which are becoming important on-ramps to the Internet.

But wireless was treated differently, Mr. Genachowski said, because it has "unique technical issues" and is at a more nascent stage of growth. He added, "Any reduction in Internet openness would be a cause for concern, as would any reduction in innovation and investment in mobile broadband applications, devices or networks that depend on Internet openness."

While wireless carriers will be able to block various apps and services, they won't be able to block basic Web sites or any apps that compete with their own voice and video products. That represents a win for Skype, the Internet phone service, which praised the F.C.C. rules on Tuesday.

The vote on the rules split along party lines, with two Democratic commissioners joining Mr. Genachowski to gain passage. Those commissioners, Michael J. Copps and Mignon Clyburn, both indicated that they wished the rules were tougher, but that, as Mr. Copps put it, "without some action today, the wheels of network neutrality would grind to a screeching halt for at least the next two years."

The two Republican commissioners, Robert M. McDowell and Meredith Baker, vocally opposed the rules as unnecessary and unjustified.

"The F.C.C. has provocatively chartered a collision course with the legislative branch," Mr. McDowell said, alluding to the complaints of Republicans in Congress. Before the F.C.C. meeting even began on Tuesday, the Senate Republican leader, Mitch McConnell, said in a statement that the Internet "should be left alone," and that his colleagues would "push back against new rules and regulations" next year.

House Votes Against 'Net Neutrality'

BY EDWARD WYATT | APRIL 8, 2011

WASHINGTON — The House of Representatives approved a measure on Friday that would prohibit the Federal Communications Commission from regulating how Internet service providers manage their broadband networks, potentially overturning a central initiative of the F.C.C. chairman, Julius Genachowski.

The action, which is less likely to pass the Senate and which President Obama has threatened to veto, is nevertheless significant because it puts half of the legislative branch on the same side of the debate as the United States Court of Appeals for the District of Columbia in restricting the F.C.C.'s authority over Internet service.

House Joint Resolution 37, which was approved by a vote of 240 to 179, was spurred by the F.C.C.'s approval in December of an order titled "Preserving the Open Internet." The order forbids the companies that provide the pipeline through which consumers gain access to the Internet from blocking a user's ability to reach legal Internet sites or to use legal applications.

But Republicans in the House maintained that the order exceeded the F.C.C.'s authority and put the government in the position of overseeing what content a consumer could see and which companies would benefit from Internet access.

"Congress has not authorized the Federal Communications Commission to regulate the Internet," said Representative Greg P. Walden, an Oregon Republican who sponsored the resolution.

The F.C.C. order "could open the Internet to regulation from all 50 states," Mr. Walden said, and was little more than the Obama administration's attempt to use the regulatory process "to make an end run around" the Court of Appeals ruling.

Representative Henry A. Waxman, a California Democrat, warned of dire consequences should the resolution be approved. "This is a bill that will end the Internet as we know it and threaten the jobs, investment and prosperity that the Internet has brought to America," Mr. Waxman said.

It is likely that Democrats in the Senate can defeat the measure, but by no means is that certain. The joint resolution was initiated under the Congressional Review Act, meaning that it cannot be filibustered and requires the support of only 30 senators to bring it to the floor.

President Obama courted Silicon Valley supporters during his campaign by promising to enact a "net neutrality" provision, as the F.C.C.'s order is known. Advisers to the president have said that he will veto the resolution; it would then take a vote by two-thirds of each house of Congress to override the veto.

In addition to opposing the F.C.C.'s order in Congress, some broadband providers, including Verizon, have said they will challenge the order in court. Those challenges can begin once the regulations become final, in a few months. Last year, the appeals court ruled that the F.C.C. did not prove it had the authority to sanction another major Internet provider, Comcast, for blocking access to the file-sharing service BitTorrent.

During the debate on Friday, each side accused the other of safeguarding the interests of big companies. Democrats said that Republicans were protecting the interests of the cable and phone company giants that are the dominant providers of broadband Internet service to American households. Those companies generally oppose the F.C.C. order, because they believe they need to be able to direct traffic on their networks as they see fit.

Republicans countered by accusing Democrats of protecting big technology companies, like Google, Amazon and Netflix, that have become successful because of the lack of Internet regulation but which now want to protect their turf from new competitors.

Each side in the debate also accused the other of adopting the position of totalitarian regimes in Iran and China by favoring limitations on Internet sites that people can view. Republicans said the F.C.C.'s

Internet order formalizes government control of the Internet, giving it the power to determine winners and losers among Internet start-ups.

Democrats, in turn, said that without the F.C.C.'s open Internet policy, broadband companies that also own content providers, like Comcast's ownership of NBC, would be free to block the Web sites of competitors. Six Democrats voted with the majority on the resolution, while two Republicans voted against the bill.

Few of the debaters raised some of the more technical issues that are at the center of the debate over broadband regulation, like specialized services and tiered rates. Specialized services, for which a broadband company uses part of its Internet pipeline to deliver dedicated services to specific customers, worry regulators who fear that companies will invest more to develop those more profitable offerings while neglecting to update basic broadband service.

Representative Lee Terry, a Nebraska Republican, said during the debate that supporters of the F.C.C.'s order wanted "to give the F.C.C. power over business plans," by restricting the ability of broadband service companies to offer tiered service, for which customers pay based on the amount of Internet bandwidth they use.

Just as a customer at a fast-food restaurant pays more for a large Coke than for a small one, Mr. Terry said, Internet companies should be free to charge customers more if they consume a greater amount of bandwidth because of heavy use of features like streaming video.

Keeping the Internet Neutral

BY EDUARDO PORTER | MAY 8, 2012

IMAGINE A NETWORK of private highways that reserved a special lane for Fords to zip through, unencumbered by all the other brands of cars trundling along the clogged, shared lanes. Think of the prices Ford could charge. Think of what would happen to innovation when building the best car mattered less than cutting a deal with the highway's owners.

A few years ago, Tim Wu, a professor at Columbia Law School and a leading thinker about the evolution of the "information economy," warned members of the House judiciary committee that this could be the fate of the Internet. Companies offering broadband access, he said, should not be allowed to discriminate among services online. If they did, the best service would not always win the day. "It's not who has a better product," he explained. "It's who can make a deal with AT&T, Verizon, Comcast or Time Warner."

That world may be right around the corner. Last month, the online video powerhouse Netflix started a political action committee to complement a budding lobbying effort in support of the idea that all content must be allowed to travel through the Internet on equal terms. Netflix is trying to build a coalition of businesses to make the case for this open access, also called network neutrality.

"Net neutrality has broad consumer and voter support," Reed Hastings, the chief of Netflix, said in an interview. "It is important for the sake of public access that the rules apply equally."

Netflix's immediate concern is Comcast, the biggest broadband provider in the country, whose cable brings the Internet to one in five connected homes. In March it announced that watching its Xfinity TV service on the Microsoft Xbox 360 would not count against subscribers' broadband data allowance of 250 gigabytes a month.

This, Mr. Hastings says, will give Comcast's television lineup an edge over rival shows streaming through the device, which will consume subscribers' data allotment. And nobody cares more than Netflix, whose movies and TV programs account for about a third of the peak online traffic.

"If I watch last night's 'S.N.L.' episode on my Xbox through the Hulu app, it eats up about one gigabyte of my cap, but if I watch that same episode through the Xfinity Xbox app, it doesn't use up my cap at all," Mr. Hastings wrote on his Facebook page. "In what way is this neutral?"

Comcast argues that its Xfinity move is not subject to the Federal Communications Commission's neutrality rules because the video travels exclusively on its network and not on the public Internet.

But the issue is not a mere business spat to be resolved between Comcast and Netflix. Comcast's data cap policies are reportedly giving Sony second thoughts about a planned Internet video service to compete against cable and satellite television. It's not even just a spat about TV.

The emerging dispute between Netflix and Comcast underscores the core weakness of the Internet economy. To reach the multitude of online services competing for your attention, you must first get through a bottleneck that is not competitive at all: high-speed broadband access.

Today, 96 percent of Americans have a choice of at most two broadband providers — a cable company and a phone provider. For consumers who desire very high speeds, cable is often the only choice — along with Verizon's FiOS and AT&T's U-verse in small pockets of the country. If given free rein, these gatekeepers could determine which services get to drive through the pipes that make up the Internet at what speeds and prices.

Costs are higher when there is little competition. If only 43 percent of American households with income under $25,000 a year have wired access into the home, it's because most of the rest cannot afford it. The cheapest available broadband package is more expensive in the United States than in 28 of the 34 industrialized countries in the

Organization for Economic Cooperation and Development, when measured in dollars per megabit of speed.

Just look at your phone or cable bill. In New York, Verizon offers its fast FiOS triple-play plan — including unlimited national calls and downloads at 25 megabits per second — for a promotional rate of $84.99 a month. In France, Iliad offers packages that include free international calls to 70 countries and a download speed of 100 megabits per second for less than $40.

There is little mystery here. About a decade ago, the government forced France Telecom to lease capacity on its wires to rivals for a regulated price, allowing competitors like Iliad to storm in. The United States took a different path: the Telecommunications Act of 1996 had opened the possibility of similar unbundling, but the F.C.C. decided against such action out of concern it would discourage investment in physical infrastructure.

The F.C.C. appears to have made the wrong call. Iliad started piggybacking on France Telecom's wires, but soon began laying wires of its own. In 2002, the United States had the sixth-highest broadband penetration among all O.E.C.D. countries. Last year it was in 15th place. Of 34 industrialized countries, the United States ranks 17th in terms of average download speeds. Among the 31 countries that have very-high-speed broadband access, the United States is more expensive, trailing only Turkey, Israel and Chile.

And a spate of deals between cable companies and Verizon Wireless to cross-sell one another's services does not bode well for competition and investment in the future. Verizon does not plan to expand its FiOS network beyond the 18 million homes it set out to reach six years ago. This suggests a market carve-up is about to take place, with Verizon focusing on wireless broadband and cable companies on wires into the home.

With fewer competitors in the way, broadband's gatekeepers will face less resistance to a strategy of carving special lanes out of the Internet.

Technology, of course, will shape competition and innovation online. Google is wiring Kansas City with fiber. If it extends that experiment, it could become a formidable competitor. Next-generation wireless may bring fast broadband to rural areas where laying fiber is unprofitable. But regulation will be crucial, too.

And right now, regulation appears weak. The F.C.C. has net neutrality rules. But the agency lost one neutrality case against Comcast in 2010, and Verizon is challenging the new rules issued in response to the ruling. The rules, moreover, have loopholes. For instance, they allow broadband providers to allocate portions of their pipes for special "managed" services.

Still, the government has a track record of keeping the telecommunications highway open. It sliced the Ma Bell monopoly into Babies, and ensured they carried one another's calls. In the era of dial-up Internet, it ensured that phone companies allowed rival Internet service providers to reach their customers.

The F.C.C. is under siege in Congress — where the phone and cable companies have unleashed their lobbying might. In March, the House passed a bill to limit the agency's ability to issue new regulations. Members of Congress might remember that government regulation was crucial for the development of the Internet we know today.

Fifty years ago, consumers were allowed to hook up only Bell telephones to their Bell phone lines. But in the 1960s, the F.C.C. and the courts forced the Bells to accept any device that didn't threaten the network. The decision unleashed a torrent of innovation — including the answering machine, the fax and the first device that allowed us to explore what would become the Internet: the modem.

Innovation online requires an open playing field, too.

CHAPTER 3

A New Chair, a Renewed Push for Net Neutrality

Despite repeated attempts to fulfill Obama's promise of instituting rules to maintain a free and fair internet, the future of net neutrality was uncertain upon the resignation of Julius Genachowski as chair of the Federal Communications Commission. The fact that his replacement, Tom Wheeler, had a background as a telecom lobbyist worried supporters of net neutrality. Nevertheless, by the end of his three years as F.C.C. chairman, Wheeler had made good on Obama's pledge to protect net neutrality, instituting strong rules to regulate and protect a democratic web.

Rebuffing F.C.C. in 'Net Neutrality' Case, Court Allows Streaming Deals

BY EDWARD WYATT | JAN. 14, 2014

WASHINGTON — Internet service providers are free to make deals with services like Netflix or Amazon allowing those companies to pay to stream their products to online viewers through a faster, express lane on the web, a federal appeals court ruled on Tuesday.

Federal regulators had tried to prevent those deals, saying they would give large, rich companies an unfair edge in reaching consumers. But since the Internet is not considered a utility under federal law, the court said, it is not subject to regulations banning the arrangements.

Some deals could come soon. In challenging the 2010 regulations at issue in the case, Verizon told the court that if not for the rules by the Federal Communications Commission, "we would be exploring those commercial arrangements."

Internet users will probably not see an immediate difference with their service. Consumer advocates, though, warned that higher costs to content providers could be passed on to the public, and called the ruling a serious blow against the concept of a free and open Internet. "It leaves consumers at the mercy of a handful of cable and phone providers that can give preferential treatment to the content they profit from," said Delara Derakhshani, policy counsel for Consumers Union.

Broadband providers that have spent billions of dollars building their networks, including Verizon, said the ruling confirmed their right to manage their networks as they saw fit. And they, too, said they were committed to an open Internet.

"Verizon has been and remains committed to the open Internet, which provides consumers with competitive choices and unblocked access to lawful websites and content when, where and how they want," the company said in a statement. "This will not change in light of the court's decision."

The ruling, in a case brought by Verizon against the F.C.C., concerns at its heart the basic question of whether Internet service is a utility of such vital importance, like telephone lines or electricity, that it needs to be regulated closely.

Although the court, the United States Court of Appeals for the District of Columbia, found that the regulations preventing the deals were invalid, it said that the commission did have some basic authority "to promulgate rules governing broadband providers' treatment of Internet traffic." It also upheld agency rules requiring broadband companies to disclose how they manage their networks.

At the least, the F.C.C. will have to try again to define its mission in the Internet age. Tom Wheeler, the agency's new chairman, said the agency might appeal the decision, but had previously voiced support for allowing Internet companies to experiment with new delivery methods and products. The rules, referred to as the Open Internet order and based on the principle of so-called net neutrality, were enacted in 2010 under the previous chairman, Julius Genachowski.

In a statement, Mr. Wheeler said he was "committed to maintaining our networks as engines for economic growth, test beds for innovative services and products, and channels for all forms of speech protected by the First Amendment."

"We will consider all available options," he added, "including those for appeal, to ensure that these networks on which the Internet depends continue to provide a free and open platform for innovation and expression, and operate in the interest of all Americans."

In 2002, the agency said Internet service should not be subject to the same rules as highly regulated utilities, which are governed by regulations on matters like how much they can charge customers and what content they can agree to carry.

DANIEL ROSENBAUM FOR THE NEW YORK TIMES

Tom Wheeler of the F.C.C. said it might appeal.

Tuesday's ruling essentially holds the F.C.C. to that determination, made when dial-up modems offered users the chance to crawl through chat rooms and to manipulate crude graphics.

Organizations that had opposed the agency's rules interpreted the Tuesday ruling as favorable to the F.C.C. Michael K. Powell, who was F.C.C. chairman in 2002 when the agency set up its Internet governance structure, said, "Today's historic court decision means that the F.C.C. has been granted jurisdiction over the Internet."

Mr. Powell, who is now president of the cable industry's chief lobbying group, said the decision would not result in significant changes in how Internet companies manage their broadband networks.

Verizon, in fact, portrayed the decision as at least a partial loss. "The court rejected Verizon's position that Congress did not give the Federal Communications Commission jurisdiction over broadband access," Randal Milch, a Verizon executive vice president and general counsel, said in a statement.

"At the same time," he said, "the court found that the F.C.C. could not impose last century's common carriage requirements on the Internet, and struck down rules that limited the ability of broadband providers to offer new and innovative services to their customers."

Judge David S. Tatel, who wrote the decision, was joined by Judge Judith W. Rogers in striking down the F.C.C. regulations but upholding the idea that the agency has "authority to enact measures encouraging the deployment of broadband infrastructure."

In a separate opinion, Judge Laurence H. Silberman agreed with the majority's reasons for striking down the F.C.C. rules but disputed its conclusion that Section 706 of the Communications Act gives the F.C.C. some legal authority over Internet service.

Much of the argument over net neutrality has been theoretical. Verizon noted in its court papers that the F.C.C. documented only four examples over six years of purported blocking of Internet content by service providers.

But the issue came into focus in the agency's review of the purchase of NBCUniversal by Comcast. As a condition of approving the deal, the F.C.C. made Comcast promise that it would abide by the Open Internet rules for seven years, even if the rules were modified by the courts.

David L. Cohen, an executive vice president at Comcast, said that the company was "comfortable with that commitment because we have not — and will not — block our customers' ability to access lawful Internet content, applications, or services. Comcast's customers want an open and vibrant Internet, and we are absolutely committed to deliver that experience."

Consumer advocacy groups, however, said the ruling was likely to accelerate the development of paid-access deals. "I would not be surprised if business development folks in I.S.P.'s around the country were now looking for ways to partner with content creators," said Michael Weinberg, acting co-president of Public Knowledge, a consumer advocacy group. The companies' goal is "to make sure their unpartnered service is bad enough that a paid partnership is attractive."

Nonsense, said one former F.C.C. commissioner. "The Internet was working beautifully before these rules were implemented," said Robert M. McDowell, a former F.C.C. commissioner who in 2010 voted against adopting the Open Internet rules. "It will thrive even more now that they have been struck down. In the meantime, ample laws already exist to protect consumers should market failures occur."

Disruptions: Paying to Travel in the Internet's Fast Lanes

BY NICK BILTON | FEB. 2, 2014

FOR A SUBJECT that sounds mind-numbingly dull, "network neutrality" is the most important issue facing the Internet since, well, the Internet.

The idea behind net neutrality is that the web material we see on our laptops and smartphones, whether from Google or a tiny little blog, should flow freely through the pipes of the Internet, regardless of origin, destination or content. No one gets special treatment.

But what if someone is willing to pay for her data to go faster? This is capitalism. Can't the people who own the pipes charge more?

The issue has come to the fore now that a federal appeals court has ruled that the Federal Communications Commission can no longer stand in the way of AT&T, Verizon and other Internet service providers that might want to create Internet express lanes.

Count on it: This battle isn't over yet. On Friday, President Obama said the F.C.C. was considering an appeal with the goal of maintaining "a free and open Internet."

The premise behind net neutrality goes back to the days of the telegraph. Even then, everything moved at pretty much the same speed. Since the 1970s, the F.C.C. has prevented telecommunications companies from playing favorites on long-distance telephone lines. And it's not as if your electric company charges you one rate for the electricity to power your refrigerator and another for the electricity to use a washing machine — or offer special, high-price options to those who want power during shutdowns.

The question is, Has the Internet become so fundamental to our lives that it is, in essence, a utility that should be subject to regulation?

For the likes of AT&T, Comcast and Verizon, the answer is no. They contend that if a Google or a Netflix wants to pay more to travel in the fast lane, let it. Customers, they say, will be better off.

DANIEL ROSENBAUM FOR THE NEW YORK TIMES

Tom Wheeler, the chairman of the Federal Communications Commission, which might appeal a ruling that limits how it regulates broadband providers.

The F.C.C. and others worry that such an arrangement would let Internet service providers play favorites and give preferential treatment to those who can pay for it. How could a nascent start-up compete with a Google or a Netflix if its content wasn't delivered as quickly or at the same quality? And what is to stop someone from outright blocking content?

Frankly, many people simply do not trust the AT&Ts and Verizons of the world.

"There's a long history of the telcos saying, 'We'll be good people, we'll act like the rules are in place,' and then six to nine months later they are breaking those rules," said Christopher Libertelli, a former senior legal adviser to the F.C.C. and now the head of global government relations at Netflix.

In 2007, for example, Comcast slowed traffic involving the BitTorrent file-sharing format, and the F.C.C. had to step in. And in 2012,

AT&T blocked people with unlimited data plans from using Apple's FaceTime video chat features unless they subscribed to a more expensive plan.

Mr. Libertelli said Netflix was already seeing instances of its service slowing in certain areas and the company could not do much about it.

In these cases and many more, the cable and telecommunication companies are blocking products that directly compete with the services they offer.

The Internet providers say customers should be allowed to decide with their wallets, switching to a competing provider if they do not agree with another's business practices. But most Americans do not have options to switch.

A 2013 F.C.C. report about competition among wired Internet service providers found that almost one-third of Americans have only one possible provider in their home with high-speed Internet that travels at six megabits a second or more. Another 37 percent of Americans have only two choices.

Susan Crawford, a visiting professor at Harvard Law School, notes in her book "Captive Audience: The Telecom Industry and Monopoly Power in the New Gilded Age" that telecoms are already making astounding profits while continuing to invest in new infrastructure. Profit at Verizon Communications has risen by double-digit percentages in recent years, pulling in more than $2.2 billion in profit during the third quarter of last year. AT&T, the second-largest American carrier after Verizon Wireless, reported profit of $3.8 billion during the same quarter.

Tim Wu, who coined the term "net neutrality," said he worried that the telecommunications companies were too big and too powerful to lose this battle.

"The F.C.C. is afraid of the companies they regulate. They are capable of being intimidated by them," said Mr. Wu, a professor at Columbia Law School. But Mr. Wu, who has written extensively about similar regulatory issues, predicts that this could backfire on the Internet service providers, leading to stricter regulation or to companies like Google calling their bluff.

"Phone and cable companies should be careful what they wish for because this could all blow up in their face," he said. "Verizon and Comcast could end up facing serious demands for money. It could be that Google will say to the telcos, 'Actually, if you want your customers to be able to reach Google, I'm afraid you're going to pay us.'"

For now, though, the wagons are circling the wagons. That is, until a line in one direction or another is breached — at which point, the future of the Internet may be changed forever.

F.C.C. Seeks a New Path on 'Net Neutrality' Rules

BY EDWARD WYATT | FEB. 19, 2014

WASHINGTON — Regulators are taking another crack at their effort to keep the web free and open, introducing new rules that would discourage Internet service providers from charging companies to stream their movies, music and other content through a faster express lane.

The proposal, unveiled by the Federal Communications Commission on Wednesday, is part of a continuing battle over the basic pipelines through which information flows on the Internet. With the latest plan, the F.C.C. is hewing close to previous efforts — albeit with some technical differences — with rules that would prevent Internet service providers from blocking any legal sites or services from consumers and would aim to restrict, but not outlaw, discrimination.

Broadband players like Verizon and Time Warner Cable have spent billions of dollars upgrading their infrastructure, and they argue that they should manage their networks as they like. They are pushing, for example, to give Netflix, Amazon and other content providers faster access to their customers at a cost.

But regulators want to prevent such deals, saying large, rich companies could have an unfair advantage. The worry is that innovation could be stifled, preventing the next Facebook or Google from getting off the ground. Consumer advocates have generally sided with regulators in the belief that Internet providers should not give preferential treatment to content companies willing to pay extra — a cost that could be passed on to customers.

The new proposal comes as the F.C.C. is considering Comcast's bid to buy Time Warner Cable. The deal, which would unite two of the nation's largest cable and broadband providers, has raised concerns that these bigger players would have the heft to strong-arm Internet content companies into paying for the right to reach customers.

Tom Wheeler, who took over the F.C.C. in November, has made so-called net neutrality a core issue for the agency. Under the latest proposal, Mr. Wheeler said that broadband companies would be subject to strict requirements to disclose their practices and would face greater enforcement efforts if they strayed from their promises.

"Preserving the Internet as an open platform for innovation and expression while providing certainty and predictability in the marketplace is an important responsibility of this agency," Mr. Wheeler said in a statement.

The plan represents a reboot of sorts for the F.C.C.

Two previous efforts were thrown out by the United States Court of Appeals for the District of Columbia Circuit, the first in a 2010 case filed by Comcast. Despite the ruling, Comcast agreed to follow the rules as a condition of its purchase of NBCUniversal. Comcast said last week that this agreement would extend to its purchase of Time Warner Cable.

In another case, brought by Verizon, a federal appeals court ruled last month that a similar set of the F.C.C.'s rules illegally treated Internet service providers as regulated utilities, like telephone companies. But the court said that the commission did have authority to oversee Internet service in ways that encourage competition.

In essence, that ruling expanded the commission's oversight, prompting the regulator to introduce the latest plan.

The main differences with the latest rules are technical, rather than substantive. In a strictly legal sense, the F.C.C. will cite another part of the law — Section 706 of the Communications Act — for its authority. Some of the rules would also be enforced case-by-case, avoiding a "bright line" regulation that the court said was so strict that it treated broadband companies like regulated telephone service.

In taking advantage of the ruling, the F.C.C. will not seek to immediately reclassify Internet service as a telecommunications service, subject to rate regulation and other oversight. Mr. Wheeler said that the commission would retain the right to do so, however, if its new rules were approved and did not appear to be working adequately. The commission also said it would not appeal the January court ruling.

One portion of the new proposal would significantly expand what are called the Open Internet rules. Mr. Wheeler said that the commission would look closely at overruling state laws that restrict the ability of cities and towns to offer broadband service to residents. That possibility was raised in a dissent to the court's recent opinion.

Consumer advocacy and public interest groups — many of which had pressed the F.C.C. to regulate broadband companies the same way as utilities — expressed cautious optimism about the commission's proposal.

"While skeptical that the FCC's initial focus on Section 706 will yield meaningful results, we are encouraged to see that the F.C.C. plans to keep its 'reclassification' proceeding open," Gene Kimmelman, president of Public Knowledge, said in a statement.

But the F.C.C.'s plan was poorly received by the agency's two Republican commissioners. Mike O'Rielly, the most recently appointed commissioner, said he was "deeply concerned by the announcement that the F.C.C. will begin considering new ways to regulate the Internet."

"As I have said before, my view is that Section 706 does not provide any affirmative regulatory authority," he added, referring to the section of the Communications Act cited by the court. "We should all fear that this provision ultimately may be used not just to regulate broadband providers, but eventually edge providers," or Internet content companies, he said.

Republican congressmen also expressed dismay. "No matter how many times the court says 'no,' the Obama administration refuses to abandon its furious pursuit of these harmful policies to put government in charge of the web," said a statement from Representative Fred Upton of Michigan, chairman of the committee that oversees the F.C.C., and Representative Greg Walden of Oregon, leader of the technology subcommittee. "These regulations are a solution in search of a problem."

But the agency has five commissioners — three of which, including Mr. Wheeler, are Democrats. So it is likely the rules will still get approved.

The F.C.C. will immediately begin accepting public comments on the outline of its new proposal, although it has not yet written the formal rules. The commission said it hoped to consider a formal set of rules by late spring or early summer.

Comcast and Netflix Reach Deal on Service

BY EDWARD WYATT AND NOAM COHEN | FEB. 23, 2014

COMCAST, the country's largest cable and broadband provider, and Netflix, the giant television and movie streaming service, announced an agreement Sunday in which Netflix will pay Comcast for faster and more reliable access to Comcast's subscribers.

The deal is a milestone in the history of the Internet, where content providers like Netflix generally have not had to pay for access to the customers of a broadband provider.

But the growing power of broadband companies like Comcast, Verizon and AT&T has given those companies increased leverage over sites whose traffic gobbles up chunks of a network's capacity. Netflix is one of those sites, accounting for nearly 30 percent of all Internet traffic at peak hours.

The agreement comes just 10 days after Comcast agreed to buy Time Warner Cable for $45 billion, an acquisition that would make Comcast the cable provider to nearly one-third of American homes and the high-speed Internet company for close to 40 percent. Federal regulators are expected to scrutinize whether that deal would thwart competition among cable and Internet providers.

It is also unclear whether the Comcast-Netflix deal violates the principles of what is known as net neutrality — where all content providers have equal and free access to consumers. People close to the deal characterize it as a common arrangement. Content companies frequently pay a middleman to carry traffic to a broadband provider, which then moves through its pipes and into a consumer's home.

In a news release announcing the deal, the companies said, "Netflix receives no preferential network treatment under the multiyear agreement." Details were not disclosed, but a person close to the companies said it involved annual payments of several million dollars.

Others, including Tim Wu, a Columbia Law School professor and advocate for net neutrality, said the interconnection agreement between Comcast and Netflix was one of the first such arrangements where a broadband provider like Comcast has extracted payment to send specific content through the "on ramp" to its network.

"This is the water in the basement for the Internet industry," Mr. Wu said, the first in what could be a flood of such arrangements. "I think it is going to be bad for consumers," he added, because such costs are often passed through to the customer.

One fear is that if such deals become common, only the wealthiest content companies will be able to afford to pay for them, which could stifle the next Netflix from ever getting off the ground.

The agreement also follows a January ruling from a federal appeals court that struck down the Federal Communications Commission's net neutrality rules, saying the agency overstepped its authority. This type of deal between Comcast and Netflix might have been forbidden under a liberal reading of the F.C.C.'s rules.

The announcement on Sunday confirmed reports that had trickled out late last week, as close watchers of Internet traffic began to detect a more direct Internet path of Netflix videos to Comcast customers.

In recent months, Netflix had reported that delivery speed of its content to Comcast subscribers had declined by more than 25 percent, resulting in frequent interruptions and delays for customers trying to stream television shows and movies delivered through Netflix. Customers of other providers, including Verizon, also reported delays.

Comcast, Verizon and other Internet service providers denied that they were playing any role in slowing down traffic. Instead, they blamed the intermediaries that Netflix used to deliver its content to Comcast on its way to consumers. They said that those middlemen — companies like Cogent Communications — were trying to shove too much data through too small a pipe.

The agreement, which is expected to be put fully into effect in the coming weeks, had been many months in the making, well before the Time Warner Cable announcement. The contours of a deal were reached after a meeting between Brian L. Roberts, chief executive of Comcast, and Reed Hastings, the chief executive of Netflix, at the International Consumer Electronics Show in Las Vegas last month, as well as the engineering teams of both companies, said sources close to the deal.

The new arrangement will deliver an "even better user experience to consumers, while also allowing for future growth in Netflix traffic," the companies said in their joint statement Sunday. Netflix will now deliver its content directly to Comcast rather than going through an intermediary.

These types of deals, known as "paid peering," are typically struck between companies that manage the plumbing of the Internet, unseen by consumers. Netflix does far more than that, offering original programming and features like TV and movie recommendations for users based on their previous choices.

Netflix will now essentially have its own on ramp to Comcast customers. That is different from paying to be moved through the pipes more quickly, a deal known as "paid prioritization" that is generally seen as a net-neutrality violation.

That the technical, arcane details of how streaming videos arrive on a customer's screen are the focus of corporate announcements and media coverage speaks to the outsize importance of Comcast and Netflix in how Americans now watch movies and television.

Craig Aaron, president of the consumer advocacy group Free Press, saw the Netflix deal as more reason to prevent Comcast from growing. "As a consumer, this is a really opaque process — being unable to really know who's paying what to whom," he said. "All you know as a consumer is that you are really paying in the end."

F.C.C., in a Shift, Backs Fast Lanes for Web Traffic

BY EDWARD WYATT | APRIL 23, 2014

WASHINGTON — The principle that all Internet content should be treated equally as it flows through cables and pipes to consumers looks all but dead.

The Federal Communications Commission said on Wednesday that it would propose new rules that allow companies like Disney, Google or Netflix to pay Internet service providers like Comcast and Verizon for special, faster lanes to send video and other content to their customers.

The proposed changes would affect what is known as net neutrality — the idea that no providers of legal Internet content should face discrimination in providing offerings to consumers, and that users should have equal access to see any legal content they choose.

The proposal comes three months after a federal appeals court struck down, for the second time, agency rules intended to guarantee a free and open Internet.

Tom Wheeler, the F.C.C. chairman, defended the agency's plans late Wednesday, saying speculation that the F.C.C. was "gutting the open Internet rule" is "flat out wrong." Rather, he said, the new rules will provide for net neutrality along the lines of the appeals court's decision.

Still, the regulations could radically reshape how Internet content is delivered to consumers. For example, if a gaming company cannot afford the fast track to players, customers could lose interest and its product could fail.

The rules are also likely to eventually raise prices as the likes of Disney and Netflix pass on to customers whatever they pay for the speedier lanes, which are the digital equivalent of an uncongested car pool lane on a busy freeway.

Consumer groups immediately attacked the proposal, saying that not only would costs rise, but also that big, rich companies with the money to pay large fees to Internet service providers would be favored over small start-ups with innovative business models — stifling the birth of the next Facebook or Twitter.

"If it goes forward, this capitulation will represent Washington at its worst," said Todd O'Boyle, program director of Common Cause's Media and Democracy Reform Initiative. "Americans were promised, and deserve, an Internet that is free of toll roads, fast lanes and censorship — corporate or governmental."

If the new rules deliver anything less, he added, "that would be a betrayal."

Mr. Wheeler rebuffed such criticism. "There is no 'turnaround in policy,'" he said in a statement. "The same rules will apply to all Internet content. As with the original open Internet rules, and consistent with the court's decision, behavior that harms consumers or competition will not be permitted."

Broadband companies have pushed for the right to build special lanes. Verizon said during appeals court arguments that if it could make those kinds of deals, it would.

Under the proposal, broadband providers would have to disclose how they treat all Internet traffic and on what terms they offer more rapid lanes, and would be required to act "in a commercially reasonable manner," agency officials said. That standard would be fleshed out as the agency seeks public comment.

The proposed rules would also require Internet service providers to disclose whether in assigning faster lanes, they have favored their affiliated companies that provide content. That could have significant implications for Comcast, the nation's largest provider of high-speed Internet service, because it owns NBCUniversal.

Also, Comcast is asking for government permission to take over Time Warner Cable, the third-largest broadband provider, and opponents of the merger say that expanding its reach as a broadband company will give Comcast more incentive to favor its own content over that of unaffiliated programmers.

Mr. Wheeler has signaled for months that the federal appeals court decision striking down the earlier rules could force the commission to loosen its definitions of what constitutes an open Internet.

Those earlier rules effectively barred Internet service providers from making deals with services like Amazon or Netflix to allow those companies to pay to stream their products to viewers through a faster, express lane on the web. The court said that because the Internet is not considered a utility under federal law, it was not subject to that sort of regulation.

Opponents of the new proposed rules said they appeared to be full of holes, particularly in seeking to impose the "commercially reasonable" standard.

"The very essence of a 'commercial reasonableness' standard is discrimination," Michael Weinberg, a vice president at Public Knowledge, a consumer advocacy group, said in a statement. "And the core of net neutrality is nondiscrimination."

Mr. Weinberg added that the commission and courts had acknowledged that it could be commercially reasonable for a broadband provider to charge a content company higher rates for access to consumers because that company's service was competitively threatening.

"This standard allows Internet service providers to impose a new price of entry for innovation on the Internet," he said.

Consumers can pay Internet service providers for a higher-speed Internet connection. But whatever speed they choose, under the new rules, they might get some content faster, depending on what the content provider has paid for.

The fight over net neutrality has gone on for at least a decade, and is likely to continue at least until the F.C.C. settles on new rules. Each of the last two times the agency has written rules, one of the Internet service providers has taken it to court to have the rules invalidated.

If anything, lobbying over the details of the new net neutrality standard is likely to increase now that the federal court has provided a framework for the F.C.C. to work from as it fills in the specifics of its regulatory authority.

The proposed rules, drafted by Mr. Wheeler and his staff, will be circulated to the agency's other four commissioners beginning on Thursday and will be released for public comment on May 15. They are likely to be put to a vote by the full commission by the end of the year.

News of the F.C.C. proposal was first reported online by The Wall Street Journal.

Top Cable Lobbyist Argues Against Broadband as Utility

BY EDWARD WYATT | APRIL 29, 2014

AMERICA'S INFRASTRUCTURE is crumbling, says Michael Powell, the chief executive of the cable industry's trade association. Roads are in poor condition, bridges are structurally deficient, drinking water systems are near the end of their useful life and portions of the electric grid suffer regular blackouts.

All of which, Mr. Powell says, proves that the country's broadband networks cannot be considered a public utility and left in the hands of government oversight.

"Because the Internet is not regulated as a public utility, it grows and thrives, watered by private capital and a light regulatory touch," Mr. Powell said Tuesday in Los Angeles at the Cable Show, the annual meeting of the National Cable & Telecommunications Association.

"It does not depend on the political process for its growth, or the extended droughts of public funding," Mr. Powell said. "This is why broadband is the fastest deploying technology in world history, reaching nearly every citizen in our expansive country."

Mr. Powell's remarks were in response to recent calls for the Federal Communications Commission to reclassify high-speed Internet service as a "common carrier," a public utilitylike network that should be subject to strict regulation.

As part of its inquiry into the future of net neutrality — the theory that consumers should have unfettered access to any legal online content, with no content being given priority over another — the F.C.C. has said that the option of reclassifying broadband service as a public utility is still on the table. That stance, agency officials say, is meant to put some pressure on broadband providers to agree to some net neutrality guidelines.

Broadband operators have opposed some of those guidelines. They say they need to be free to make deals that will improve service, including charging certain content providers for access to a special express lane to cut through broadband congestion and reach consumers more quickly.

The F.C.C., whose two previous attempts to devise net neutrality rules were struck down by a federal appeals court, is preparing to release a new net neutrality proposal that agency officials say will allow broadband companies to make those kinds of deals with content providers, a position strongly opposed by many consumer advocacy organizations.

While the Internet and broadband systems were built "with the help of the government," Mr. Powell said, "they have suffered terribly chronic underinvestment." In 2002, when Mr. Powell was chairman of the F.C.C., the agency voted to regulate cable-modem broadband service as a lightly regulated "information service" rather than as a "common carrier."

"It is the Internet's essential nature that fuels a very heated policy debate that the network cannot be left in private hands and should instead be regulated as a public utility, following the example of the Interstate highway system, the electric grid and drinking water," Mr. Powell said. "The intuitive appeal of this argument is understandable, but the potholes visible through your windshield, the shiver you feel in a cold house after a snowstorm knocks out the power and the water main breaks along your commute should restrain one from embracing the illusory virtues of public utility regulation."

Defending the Open Internet

BY JEFF SOMMER | MAY 10, 2014

THE FUTURE OF THE INTERNET — which means the future of communications, culture, free speech and innovation — is up for grabs.

The Federal Communications Commission is making decisions that may determine how open the Internet will be, who will profit most from it and whether start-ups will face new barriers that will make it harder for ideas to flourish.

Tim Wu, 41, a law professor at Columbia University, isn't a direct participant in the rule making, but he is influencing it. A dozen years ago, building on the work of more senior scholars, Mr. Wu developed a concept that is now a generally accepted norm. Called "net neutrality," short for network neutrality, it is essentially this: The cable and telephone companies that control important parts of the plumbing of the Internet shouldn't restrict how the rest of us use it.

Most everyone embraces net neutrality, yet the debate over how to accomplish it is so volatile that more than a million signatures have been filed protesting F.C.C. regulations that haven't even been proposed yet. (They may be released in draft form on Thursday.)

What makes the current debate so contentious is that the F.C.C. has signaled its intention to grant cable and telephone companies the right to charge content companies like Netflix, Google, Yahoo or Facebook for speeding up transmissions to people's homes. And this is happening as the F.C.C. is considering whether to bless the merger of Comcast and Time Warner Cable, which could put a single company in control of the Internet pipes into 40 percent of American homes.

In other words, these arcane matters of engineering and jurisprudence stir people up because they appear to violate net neutrality.

"Sometimes what everybody thinks about the law is more important than what the law itself says," Mr. Wu told me recently in his Columbia office. "I think that's what's happened with net neutrality. It's become

TINA FINEBERG FOR THE NEW YORK TIMES

Tim Wu, the law professor at Columbia University who came up with the term "net neutrality," has argued that the concept be protected by law and regulation.

a kind of norm of behavior, what you can and can't appropriately do with the Internet. It's got to be open. Except for legitimate purposes like protecting the network itself, there shouldn't be discrimination against one form of content or another or one provider or another. And people generally accept that. Until now, the idea in a way has been more important than what the regulations have actually said."

But what the law says is important, even paramount, and Mr. Wu is one of the most influential voices arguing that net neutrality be fully protected by law and regulation, which, in his view, means treating the Internet like a regulated utility, for the good of all. That remedy may not happen immediately. But his opinion is nonetheless sought out by rule makers.

What got him to this point of influence and authority, besides his creative legal scholarship, was firsthand experience in Silicon Valley during the wildest days of the dot-com era. And a depressing afternoon at an Atlanta strip joint.

'A PERPETUAL FRONTIER'

On a rainy May afternoon, Mr. Wu, attired in academic casual, sat in his cluttered office discussing the state of the Internet and his place in it.

A child of peripatetic scientists, he was born in Washington and spent formative years in Basel, Switzerland, and Toronto. His father, born in Taiwan, was a noted immunologist. He died in 1981, when Mr. Wu was 8. His mother, who moved from London to Canada as a child, is an immunologist at York University in Toronto.

Thanks to his mother's farsighted purchase of an Apple II computer in 1982, Tim Wu says proudly that he became something of a geek. "That computer changed our lives, my brother's and mine," he said.

In high school, Tim Wu got a part-time job writing software, while operating an online bulletin board, "the main purpose of which was to move around pirated software," he said. "Hey, it was a different time." His younger brother, David, is now a computer game software developer.

A biochemistry major at McGill University, Mr. Wu was headed toward a career in "the family business — science," when, he noted wryly, "I had a sort of rebellion." It took the form of an application to Harvard Law School, where he spent the next three years. But he didn't really know why he was at Harvard until he wandered into a cyberlaw class taught by Lawrence Lessig, an early advocate of an open Internet. "I didn't know what cyberlaw was exactly, but it seemed cool," Mr. Wu said. "Larry gave me my calling."

Mr. Lessig said he recognized that Mr. Wu was "unusually gifted" and helped arrange two clerkships for him. (Several years later, Mr. Lessig recommended that another student receive the same clerkships, and she did. Her name is Kathryn Judge. She is also a Columbia law professor and Mr. Wu's wife.)

For one year, Mr. Wu worked for Richard A. Posner, a federal appellate court judge, influential University of Chicago law professor, prolific author and blogger. "Richard Posner is a kind of law demigod," Mr. Wu said. "He didn't really need a clerk. He wrote everything on his own. But he wanted someone to be his critic — to match wits with him intellectually, to fight with him and tell him why he was wrong."

Judge Posner encouraged Mr. Wu to be a contrarian — and to find an independent road in the broad territory between heavy-handed government interference and free-market anarchy.

In 1999 and 2000, Mr. Wu served as a clerk to Justice Stephen G. Breyer of the Supreme Court. There he played a different role. Justice Breyer's law clerks, Mr. Wu said, were expected to find out what the other justices were contemplating. "One of Breyer's favorite things was to ask, 'What does Sandra think?,'" referring to Sandra Day O'Connor, who was often the pivotal vote until she retired in 2006. "He believed he had a big job trying to defend the middle ground in the court — to form a caucus of reasonable adults."

In 2000, as Mr. Wu's clerkship came to a close, the country was infected with dot-com fever. And even at the Supreme Court, he caught a case of it. With his legal pedigree and programming skills, he was in high demand. He opted for a high-risk, high-reward opportunity: a marketing job with a start-up firm in Silicon Valley called Riverstone Networks. The company, he said, "promised to make us all rich."

Instead, it made him disillusioned. He says he was appalled by the business practices around him. "Network neutrality came out of the bad things there," he said.

The company sold industrial-size Internet routers that were being used, Mr. Wu recalls, "to block and prioritize Internet traffic, to discriminate against traffic, basically, to do many of the things that I think companies on the Internet shouldn't be doing." He went to China for the company and found that the equipment he was dealing in was of interest to the Chinese for its potential to abet censorship.

"Helping the Chinese government censor dissidents wasn't the way I wanted to spend the rest of my life," he said. "It hit me that we

TINA FINEBERG FOR THE NEW YORK TIMES

Mr. Wu says the Internet should be regulated like a utility for the good of everyone.

weren't on the good side there." The idea of net neutrality grew, in part, because "I had personal experience of violations of it," he said.

That was only part of the problem. The company's top executives were engaging in activities that the Securities and Exchange Commission and federal prosecutors said were improper. His immediate boss, Andrew Feldman, ultimately pleaded guilty to a felony count of violating internal accounting controls, and Mr. Feldman and four other top executives agreed to an S.E.C. settlement in a complaint accusing them of a scheme to defraud investors by misstating revenues.

Mr. Wu was untouched by the investigations, but said he had known that things weren't right.

It all crystallized for him on Sept. 12, 2001 — the day after the 9/11 attacks. He was stranded in Atlanta at a trade show with other company employees. Their business engagements were canceled because of the attacks, and, with no other plans, his colleagues decided to go to a strip club. On such a solemn day, the tawdry revelry repelled him.

"I wondered how I'd gotten there," he recalls. "I realized that what we'd been doing all those months was abhorrent." He had been living in a world based on nothing but money, he said, and saw that "the idea that the private sector, the free market, on its own has all the solutions is just a myth." He added: "When it's just about money, there are no values."

He looked for a way out and got a job teaching law at the University of Virginia. But the Internet preoccupied him. "I thought of it as a kind of perpetual frontier, the place where everyone gets a shot, where the underdogs have a chance. The Internet has been that. And I wanted some principles that would keep it that way."

He got back in touch with Mr. Lessig, who encouraged him in May 2002 to put his thoughts down on paper. The result was a sparkling memo, "A Proposal for Network Neutrality," that asked: "What principle can balance the legitimate interests of broadband carriers in administering their networks with the danger of harm to new application markets? And how can such a principle be translated into both clear legal guidelines and the practice of network design?" The answer was in the title: a new creation called network neutrality. Mr. Lessig began sending the paper to his contacts the next month.

Mr. Wu's ideas spread, reaching top staff members at the F.C.C., who brought them to the attention of Michael Powell, then the commission chairman.

"I was convinced by Tim Wu's ideas," Mr. Powell said in an interview last week. He cited Mr. Wu in a major speech in 2004, calling on Internet providers to refrain from blocking or restricting data or applications available to consumers. He asked consumers to "challenge their broadband providers to live up to these standards and to let the commission know how the industry is doing." In 2005, the F.C.C. enjoined Madison River Communications, a telephone company, from blocking phone service over the Internet. In essence, Mr. Powell told me, "the F.C.C. made network neutrality the law of the land."

THE 'COMMON CARRIER' DEBATE

The argument today is not so much whether net neutrality is a good concept — most people agree that it is — but what it means in practice.

Mr. Lessig and Mr. Wu both say Mr. Powell was effective in maintaining an open Internet. He used a very light regulatory hand — and this has left some issues unresolved to this day. He decided that the Internet was "an information service" and not a "common carrier." This semantic difference is crucial. Common carriers, like phone companies, are more tightly regulated, and while Mr. Powell prohibited the arbitrary blocking or setting of priorities for Internet traffic, he did so without invoking the F.C.C.'s authority over common carriers, which is embodied in Title II of the Communications Act of 1934.

This point has haunted the F.C.C. ever since. In January, the United States Court of Appeals for the District of Columbia Circuit struck down open Internet rules that had been in place since 2010. The court said the F.C.C. had regulated broadband carriers as though they were common carriers, yet the agency hadn't designated them as such.

Congress could intervene, but has not done so. One reason for his original decision, Mr. Powell said in the interview, was that the Internet needed enormous capital investment, which would have been deterred by tighter regulations. "If I thought Congress wanted to throw $10 billion or $20 billion or $30 billion a year into building up the infrastructure, I'd be willing to have a conversation about how to regulate such a system."

Today, Mr. Powell speaks as the head of the cable industry's trade organization. "Now that private markets have created a system with certain expectations on return of capital," he said, "it would be wrong, from many perspectives, to change the rules and confiscate what has been a public good."

Mr. Wu and his allies argue that broadband carriers — basically the telephone and cable companies — do, in fact, function as common carriers. In their view, the Internet is increasingly crucial to the economy, society and the political system, and its openness to all comers needs to be enforced by the F.C.C., which should invoke its full authority under Title II.

Netflix has already begun making deals with Comcast and Verizon Communications to ensure swift transmissions from its servers to their broadband networks, and with the new F.C.C. proposals, priority service might be permitted through the "last mile" of these networks — that is, through the broadband networks into people's homes. Mr. Wu says both sorts of commercial prioritization should be regulated under Title II.

Andrew McLaughlin, the chief executive of Digg, a news collection site, said last week that he was worried that if big companies were allowed to buy priority service on the Internet, "it will be harder for two guys in a garage with a great idea to innovate and get their ideas out and compete." Mr. McLaughlin was an adviser to President Obama on these issues from his election in November 2008 through 2010. Mr. McLaughlin's words echoed comments made by the president in February 2010 in an interview on YouTube.

"I'm a big believer in net neutrality," Mr. Obama said in that interview. "We're getting pushback, obviously from some of the bigger carriers, obviously who would like to charge more fees and extract more money from wealthier customers, but we think that runs counter to the whole spirit of openness that has made the Internet such a powerful engine not only for economic growth but also for the generation of ideas and creativity."

Many companies, including content providers like Netflix and Yahoo; social media sites like Facebook, Twitter and Reddit; search sites like Google and Microsoft's Bing; and e-commerce companies like Amazon, say they worry that the F.C.C. might give "broadband gatekeepers" control.

In a letter to the F.C.C. last week, these companies and many others said the new rule making "represents a grave threat to the Internet." Cable and telephone industries respond that it is in their own interests to keep the Internet open. The main question, they say, is whether content providers will help pay for the cost of operating and building the network. "That's just a financial issue," Mr. Powell said. "It's not a question of principle."

Some scholars say there are merits to the F.C.C..'s apparent approach. Philip J. Weiser, dean of the University of Colorado Law School, said, common-carrier regulation "is not a panacea." If the F.C.C. were to use it, he said, there would most likely be years of litigation. Even if the classification withstood a legal challenge, he said, it might not improve the situation. Priority service would presumably be permitted for a "reasonable fee" so long as that fee was offered to everybody.

"It's like FedEx," he said. "You pay a certain amount for overnight delivery and a certain amount for two-day delivery. You could end up with something like that for the Internet."

The agency's evident strategy is fraught with problems, and there has been dissension in its own ranks. "The F.C.C. appears to be attempting to thread a needle," said Christopher S. Yoo, a law professor at the University of Pennsylvania. It wants to avoid invoking Title II, he said, while adding enough conditions to a standard of "commercial reasonableness" for prioritizing Internet transmissions to satisfy the courts as well as the fiercest net-neutrality advocates. "I don't think we'll know for a while whether they can succeed."

Mr. Wu views the current battles as the latest in a long cycle. His book, "The Master Switch: The Rise And Fall of Information Empires," describes how the F.C.C., as a weak overseer of the old AT&T telephone monopoly, often acted less in the public interest than to promote the interests of the company. Mergers like the one now proposed between Comcast and Time Warner Cable, which he opposes, could create new behemoths that might overwhelm the F.C.C. Yet he says the agency should persevere, using the most powerful weapons at its disposal, which include Title II.

He says media companies will combine and grow — until they grow too large and start to fragment, and are replaced by more dynamic companies, in an endless cycle. In his book, he cites "The Romance of the Three Kingdoms," the classic Chinese novel: "An empire long united must divide; an empire long divided must unite." But when this process takes place in the modern world, he says, government regulators must protect the public interest.

Lawmakers Introduce Bill to Ban Paid Prioritization

BY EDWARD WYATT | JUNE 17, 2014

WASHINGTON — Democratic members of both houses of Congress introduced legislation Tuesday that would ban Internet service providers from charging content companies for faster or more direct connections to Internet service subscribers.

Senator Patrick J. Leahy, a Vermont Democrat, and Representative Doris Matsui, a California Democrat, filed bills in their respective chambers that would ban so-called paid prioritization — deals similar to the recent agreement that allows Netflix to connect directly to Comcast's system to avoid network congestion.

GABRIELLA DEMCZUK/THE NEW YORK TIMES

Senator Patrick J. Leahy, a Vermont Democrat, introduced legislation that would ban deals like Netflix's arrangement to connect directly to Comcast's system to avoid network congestion.

The legislators said that the bill "would help prevent the creation of a two-tiered Internet system, ensuring start-ups and entrepreneurs have access to the marketplace and ensuring consumers can access all content equally."

With no Republican co-sponsors as yet, the proposal will most likely have a hard time making it through the House of Representatives.

The bills are the latest development in a fervent public debate over net neutrality, the concept that all Internet traffic should be treated equally as it moves through networks on its way to a consumer.

Last week, the chairman of the Federal Communications Commission said the agency was opening an inquiry into those types of deals, which critics contend would divide the Internet into fast and slow lanes.

Internet-service providers like Comcast and Verizon, which also struck a deal with Netflix, say that their agreements involve interconnection of networks and are not covered by the concept of net neutrality. Net neutrality, they say, applies only to what is known as the last mile — the Internet service provider's pipe to a consumer.

The F.C.C. also is collecting public comment on proposals for how to ensure an open Internet, and more than 20,000 comments have been registered at the agency. Two previous attempts by the agency to complete such rules were struck down by a federal appeals court.

In its proposals, the F.C.C. says that interconnection agreements are not covered by its proposed rules. But the commission also asked for comment on whether paid-prioritization deals should be disallowed.

"Americans are speaking loud and clear," Mr. Leahy said. "They want an Internet that is a platform for free expression and innovation, where the best ideas and services can reach consumers based on merit rather than based on a financial relationship with a broadband provider."

Obama Asks F.C.C. to Adopt Tough Net Neutrality Rules

BY EDWARD WYATT | NOV. 10, 2014

WASHINGTON — In his most direct effort yet to influence the debate about the Internet's future, President Obama said on Monday that a free and open Internet was as critical to Americans' lives as electricity and telephone service and should be regulated like those utilities to protect consumers.

The Federal Communications Commission, Mr. Obama said, needs to adopt the strictest rules possible to prevent broadband companies from blocking or intentionally slowing down legal content and from allowing content providers to pay for a fast lane to reach consumers. That approach, he said, demands thinking about both wired and wireless broadband service as a public utility.

"For almost a century, our law has recognized that companies who connect you to the world have special obligations not to exploit the monopoly they enjoy over access into and out of your home or business," Mr. Obama, who is traveling in Asia, said in a statement and a video on the White House website. "It is common sense that the same philosophy should guide any service that is based on the transmission of information — whether a phone call or a packet of data."

The president's move was widely interpreted as giving political support to Tom Wheeler, the F.C.C. chairman. Mr. Wheeler is close to settling on a plan to protect an open Internet, often known as net neutrality, and Mr. Obama's statement could push him to adopt a more aggressive approach. Any set of rules needs three votes from the five-member commission, which now has three Democrats and two Republicans.

The debate may hinge on whether Internet access is considered a necessity, like electricity, or more of an often-costly option, like cable TV.

The proposal was hailed by Internet content companies like Netflix, Democrats in Congress and consumer advocacy groups. But the leading providers of Internet access, increasingly dependent on revenue from broadband subscriptions, quickly denounced the proposal. Republicans and some investment groups also spoke out against the plan, saying the regulation was heavy-handed and would kill online investment and innovation.

The F.C.C.'s previous rules for net neutrality were struck down in January by a federal appeals court, leaving the commission in search of new rules. In May, the commission released a proposal that would maintain a light regulatory touch, which Mr. Obama said was not strong enough.

Mr. Wheeler, who was appointed by Mr. Obama, said he agreed with the president that "the Internet must remain an open platform for free expression, innovation and economic growth." But he stopped short of promising to follow the president's recommendation, saying more time was needed to consider options and adopt an approach that could "withstand any legal challenges it may face."

As an independent agency, the F.C.C. does not directly answer to the president. It answers more to Congress, which controls its budget and the laws under which it operates. Several efforts to enact net neutrality legislation over the last decade have failed to advance.

While Mr. Obama has long offered vocal support on the idea of net neutrality, he has been more opaque about how it should be achieved through policy.

In the last six months, almost four million people have sent comments about net neutrality to the F.C.C., the vast majority of them part of an organized campaign supporting strong rules. And in September, representatives from the websites Etsy, Kickstarter and Vimeo, among others, met with Megan J. Smith, Mr. Obama's chief technology officer, and other senior officials to ask the president to lean on the F.C.C. to impose the stricter rules that would treat broadband as a public utility. Internet content companies fear that if broadband providers can charge content companies for premium access to customers, start-ups and other small companies will be shut out.

A week ago, after floating a proposal for a hybrid approach that would classify part of broadband service as a public utility, Mr. Wheeler was warned by his aides that numerous legal issues could thwart his approach.

Last Thursday, Jeffrey D. Zients, the director of the National Economic Council, a White House agency that advises Mr. Obama, informed Mr. Wheeler of the president's intention to urge tough net neutrality rules, officials said.

By weighing in forcefully now, officials said, the president hopes that his voice will add to the pressure on the F.C.C.

But broadband companies like Verizon, which successfully challenged the F.C.C.'s last net neutrality rules, said that the president's plan was unacceptable.

And companies that make the routers and servers that are used to build the Internet backbone, represented by the Telecommunications Industry Association, said they "strongly urge regulators to refrain from reclassification that will guarantee harm to consumers, the economy and the very technologies we're trying to protect."

Shares of Comcast and Time Warner Cable, the country's two largest wired broadband Internet providers, fell about 4 percent on Monday. Shares of Verizon fell slightly, while AT&T and CenturyLink rose in a market that ended marginally higher. Shares of Google, Netflix and other content providers advanced.

Republican leaders also objected to Mr. Obama's proposal, including Senator John Thune of South Dakota, who is in line to take over the chairmanship of the Senate Commerce Committee in the Republican-controlled Senate next year.

Mr. Thune said the effort "would turn the Internet into a government-regulated utility and stifle our nation's dynamic and robust Internet sector with rules written nearly 80 years ago for plain old telephone service" — referring to the Communications Act of 1934, which created the F.C.C. to regulate wire and radio communications, including common carriers like telephone service.

Specifically, Mr. Obama has proposed reclassifying Internet service — both wired and wireless — as a Title II telecommunications service under the Communications Act. That would allow the F.C.C. to write rules that would forbid blocking of legal content and discrimination by a broadband company against any provider of content.

But Title II does not by itself ban the ability of a broadband provider to charge a content company for a preferred service.

"You need strong rules, and you probably use some of the other powers of the commission to augment those rules," said Gene Kimmelman, president of Public Knowledge, a consumer advocacy group.

Title II also carries with it the possibility of regulating rates, but Mr. Obama asked the F.C.C. to refrain "from rate regulation and other provisions less relevant to broadband services."

But forbearance from portions of the law are not always easy, because Title II has upward of 1,000 requirements, said Robert M. McDowell, a former F.C.C. commissioner. "As a legal matter," Mr. McDowell said, "it would be very difficult for the F.C.C. to subject the Internet to common-carrier regulation while at same time forbearing from the vast majority of Title II."

Once the regulation is challenged in court, he said, "That is what makes this whole idea very wobbly."

MICHAEL D. SHEAR AND JULIE HIRSCHFELD DAVIS CONTRIBUTED REPORTING.

In Net Neutrality Push, Internet Giants on the Sidelines

FARHAD MANJOO | NOV. 11, 2014

SILICON VALLEY'S giant companies have been quiet lately on the question of whether the government should protect an open Internet, which they've previously argued is vital to innovation. Don't count on them staking out a stronger position even though President Obama has stepped into the fray, and Washington looks to be gearing up for an epic battle over the rules that govern the Internet.

On Monday, Mr. Obama offered his support for a strict set of rules that, among other proscriptions, would prohibit broadband carriers from blocking online content, and would restrict them from giving priority access over their lines to companies that pay an extra fee.

In another era, the White House's position might have elicited squeals of joy from the technology giants, which have long maintained that the future of innovation online depends on such strict net neutrality rules. But Google, which was once the industry's most ardent supporter of net neutrality, and Facebook, which could mobilize millions of supporters through its service, both declined to comment on Mr. Obama's position.

Instead, they joined a supportive statement put out by the Internet Association, a trade group that represents a coalition of technology companies, including Amazon, eBay, Yahoo, Twitter and PayPal.

The muted response was not surprising. Since January, when a federal appeals court threw out the Federal Communications Commission's rules on net neutrality, broadband companies like Comcast, Verizon and AT&T have mounted a full-court public and legislative fight against any new round of regulations that would curb how they manage their networks. Their rival giants in the tech industry haven't put up much of a fight.

Large Internet businesses have written a few letters to regulators in support of the issue and have participated in the back-channel lobbying effort, but they have not joined online protests, or otherwise moved to mobilize their users in favor of new rules.

Why not? They may be too big to bother with an issue that primarily affects the smallest Internet companies. And that is a shame.

The White House's proposal is seen as the beginning of what could be a heated battle on net neutrality. Supporters are gearing up for a fierce fight at the F.C.C. and in the incoming majority-Republican Congress. In other words, it's going to get ugly — and now, more than ever, reinforcements from tech giants would help the neutrality cause.

Net neutrality rules would keep broadband lines neutral of the Internet providers' business interests. Say, for instance, you get high-speed Internet service from Comcast. Without strong rules, advocates say, Comcast could favor certain websites or videos on the lines coming into your home — perhaps those from TV networks it owns, or from outside companies from which it has exacted a fee for access to a special "fast lane" on the Internet.

If that were to happen, proponents of the rules say, it's obvious which companies would suffer most: the Internet's newest and least powerful businesses. The giants, meanwhile, would escape relatively unscathed.

"If you have bad rules, the ones who pay the price are the smallest companies," said Julie Samuels, the executive director of Engine, a group that has been pushing for network neutrality rules. "Once you're as large as Google or Facebook, you can afford to pay."

For much of the year, that dynamic has been playing out. Last September, web companies in favor of net neutrality supported an effort to slow down many well-known sites in order to demonstrate how web users would be harmed if net neutrality rules were not enacted.

"Our campaign was driven by a tight consortium of mostly New York City-based companies," said Yancey Strickler, the chief executive and co-founder of Kickstarter, which took part in the effort, joined by Etsy, Tumblr, Vimeo and Netflix, among other upstarts.

But the Internet's biggest names — Google, Facebook, Twitter, Microsoft, Amazon and Apple — sat out the protest. If you pulled up Google's search results or Facebook's News Feed on Internet Slowdown Day, you would not have noticed anything amiss.

"I'm not sure what it is that kept the bigger West Coast companies out of this publicly, but ultimately I'm concerned with the outcome," Mr. Strickler said. "If this campaign continues to go on, we would love to see Google and Facebook and Apple and Amazon step forward to talk about the rights of their communities and the future of the web."

Still, the campaign has been remarkably effective despite the absence of web giants.

"The fact that not every company could hide behind Google made some companies more willing to speak out," said Craig Aaron, the president of the advocacy group Free Press. "In 2010, when Google was more out front on this, a lot of companies were willing to let them take the shots."

Pro-neutrality organizers managed to whip up a record-setting 3.7 million public comments to the F.C.C. regarding the issue, most of them in favor of a strong proposal. They see Mr. Obama's statement as a direct response to the outpouring of public support.

In some ways, the absence of large tech companies allowed advocates to paint the issue as something of a David versus Goliath battle. Here the broadband behemoths were not pitted against faceless Silicon Valley giants, but against little guys like Etsy and Kickstarter, as well as against their fiercely loyal users.

"Part of why we're so active in this issue is that we are serving as a voice box for what our users want," said Ari Shahdadi, the general counsel of Tumblr, the blogging service that was bought last year by Yahoo but still operates like a freewheeling start-up.

Consider, for instance, the pro-neutrality argument offered by Etsy, which is a marketplace for handmade items. Most Etsy sellers are women who have set up shop in their homes. “The Internet has allowed them to compete with big brands in the global marketplace, and we felt that was under threat,” said Althea Erickson, the company’s public policy director.

Ms. Erickson pointed out that Etsy makes low margins, taking just 3.5 percent of every transaction. It would not have been able to pay for priority access if broadband companies ever created a fast lane online. “And we know that speed really matters,” she said. “Delays of even fractions of a second result in dropped revenue for our users.”

In portraying the issue as a problem for their users, the smaller companies highlight the most important constituency for network neutrality: people like Etsy sellers, Tumblr bloggers and Kickstarter entrepreneurs, people who use the Internet to circumvent the world’s entrenched power structures.

Google, Facebook, Twitter, Amazon and other large companies — with their tens of millions of American users — could mount similar campaigns on a wider scale.

They could, for example, explain how we’d all have lost out if broadband companies were free to block messaging apps like WhatsApp, now owned by Facebook, because it posed a threat to carriers’ exorbitant SMS-texting prices. Or how fledgling comedians on YouTube might never have been discovered if the video site, now owned by Google, had been required to pay an access fee in its earliest days.

“Their users really, really care about this issue,” said Mr. Aaron, of Free Press. “I hope they’d recognize that, as the smaller companies have recognized that. We’d welcome their support.”

Obama and Scalia, United on Broadband as a Utility

BY EDWARD WYATT | NOV. 13, 2014

WASHINGTON — The number of issues on which President Obama agrees with Justice Antonin Scalia probably could be counted on one hand. But one such agreement is a doozy — that broadband Internet service should be regulated as a utility.

President Obama on Monday urged the Federal Communications Commission to reverse a decision it made in 2002 that high-speed Internet service shouldn't be treated as a "telecommunications service" — that is, a sort of utility-like telephone service — under Title II of the Communications Act of 1934.

At the time, the F.C.C. decided that the Internet had a better chance to thrive if broadband were classified as an "information service," making it subject to a lighter regulatory touch under Title I of the Communications Act.

The commission reasoned that Internet service providers offered not just the transmission of digits, but rather an integrated service that also offered the capability for manipulating and storing information.

That judgment was affirmed by the United States Supreme Court in 2005, in National Cable & Telecommunications Association v. Brand X Internet Services, No. 04-277. The court ruled 6-3 in the case that the F.C.C. correctly decided that the changed market conditions under which the Internet was developing warranted different treatment of broadband.

Republicans have repeatedly seized on that ruling this week in warning the F.C.C. and President Obama against reclassifying broadband as a Title II service.

But attached to the Supreme Court opinion is a strong dissent written by Justice Scalia, one that puts him on the same side with President Obama.

The gist of the majority's opinion was that broadband companies did not "offer" a telecommunications service by itself to consumers. Rather, the majority wrote, the service was integrated within more complex services and not offered on a stand-alone basis.

Justice Scalia disagreed, joined by two others, Justice Ruth Bader Ginsburg and Justice David H. Souter, who is now retired.

"It seems to me," Justice Scalia wrote, "that the analytic problem pertains not really to the meaning of 'offer,' but to the identity of what is offered."

"It would be odd to say that a car dealer is in the business of selling steel or carpets because the cars he sells include both steel frames and carpeting," he wrote. "Nor does the water company sell hydrogen, nor the pet store water (though dogs and cats are largely water at the molecular level)."

What is sometimes true, however, is not always true, Justice Scalia said, and the basis of broadband Internet service is the transmission of digits from one point to another — in other words, a telecommunications service.

"The pet store may have a policy of selling puppies only with leashes," he wrote, "but any customer will say that it does offer puppies — because a leashed puppy is still a puppy, even though it is not offered on a 'stand-alone' basis."

Most people in the Internet world expect that whatever path the F.C.C. takes will end up back in court. If the dispute makes it to the Supreme Court, broadband might make for strange bedfellows.

Obama's Net Neutrality Bid Divides Civil Rights Groups

BY EDWARD WYATT | DEC. 7, 2014

WASHINGTON — When President Obama laid out his vision for strict regulation of Internet access last month, he was voicing views thought to be held by many at the most liberal end of the Democratic Party.

A few days later, however, the N.A.A.C.P., the National Urban League and the Rainbow/PUSH Coalition sent representatives, including the Rev. Jesse L. Jackson, to tell Tom Wheeler, chairman of the Federal Communications Commission, that they thought Mr. Obama's call to regulate broadband Internet service as a utility would harm minority communities by stifling investment in underserved areas and entrenching already dominant Internet companies.

Their displeasure should not be read as a sign that most civil rights organizations were unhappy with Mr. Obama's plan, however. When it comes to the details of Internet regulation, groups that otherwise have much common ground simply don't see eye to eye.

ColorofChange.org, a black political coalition, and the National Hispanic Media Coalition, for example, support treating Internet access as an essential service like electricity or water, as Mr. Obama proposed, while the League of United Latin American Citizens opposes it.

"The civil rights community is like every sector anywhere. While from the outside it seems like a monolith, it is not," said Cheryl A. Leanza, a policy adviser for the United Church of Christ Office of Communication. Though she was part of the 11-member group that included Mr. Jackson, she asked the chairman to embrace the president's plan.

The debate is but one slice of a huge campaign to lobby the five F.C.C. commissioners as they weigh net neutrality, the concept that all Internet traffic should be treated equally, and whether to reclassify broadband as a more heavily regulated service.

Since 2002, broadband has been classified as a Title I information service under the Telecommunications Act of 1996, meaning that the F.C.C. lightly regulates it. Title II services include "common carriers" like telephone companies, whose rates the F.C.C. can regulate and whose business plans often require the commission's approval.

In May, Mr. Wheeler made a proposal that would allow companies to pay Internet providers to give them a "fast lane" to consumers. Mr. Wheeler is against that practice, known as paid prioritization, and he said his proposal would discourage it. But the regulatory outline released by the F.C.C. would still allow for paid prioritization in some circumstances, a loophole that was seized on by opponents.

President Obama urged the F.C.C. to reclassify broadband as a Title II service, which would generally give the commission the authority to prohibit broadband providers from blocking or discriminating against legal online content.

In the four weeks since Mr. Obama's move, over 100 companies, industry groups and coalitions have met with commissioners and their staffs. At least 67 of those groups have met with Mr. Wheeler himself — nearly four a day, on average. Included in those meetings have been civil rights groups with surprisingly divergent views.

The unusual alignments can also be seen in urban governments. The cities of Baltimore, Chicago, Los Angeles and San Francisco sent representatives to meet with Mr. Wheeler's advisers to say they agreed with tight regulation, but that view is opposed by the National Organization of Blacks in Government.

"I think we're all on board with the values embedded in what President Obama said, things like accelerating broadband deployment and adoption," said Nicol Turner-Lee, vice president of the Minority Media and Telecommunications Council and a member of the group including Mr. Jackson that met with the F.C.C. chairman. "The question is, will we be able to solve these issues by going so far with stringent regulation?"

Some of the groups that oppose Title II designation, like the Urban League and the League of United Latin American Citizens, have received contributions from organizations affiliated with Internet

T.J. KIRKPATRICK FOR THE NEW YORK TIMES

Nicol Turner-Lee, vice president of the Minority Media and Telecommunications Council, in her Washington office last week.

service providers, like the Comcast Foundation, the charitable organization endowed by Comcast. Parts of the Rainbow/PUSH Coalition's annual symposium on civil rights were conducted last week at Comcast's offices in Washington.

But those organizations say that the donations or sponsorships do not influence their positions. "We get support from people on all sides of the issue, including Google and Facebook," said Brent A. Wilkes, national executive director of the League of United Latin American Citizens. "We don't let any of them influence our position."

Several of those favoring Title II, meanwhile, have received funding from organizations affiliated with companies that support stronger regulation. The National Hispanic Media Coalition conducts events that are sponsored in part by companies like Google and Facebook. A trade organization sponsored by those and other Internet companies, the Internet Association, supports a shift to stricter regulation.

Jessica Gonzalez, executive vice president of the National Hispanic Media Coalition, said her organization also received support from Comcast for some of its programs. "There is a clear separation between our policy work and who funds us," she said.

One of the primary disagreements among the civil rights groups is over a practice known as "zero rating," in which an Internet service provider makes a deal with a content provider like Facebook or Spotify to allow consumers unlimited access to that service without its counting against a cap on data usage. Because zero-rating plans are most common among mobile broadband providers, those plans could particularly affect minority communities, Ms. Turner-Lee said, which are more likely to depend on mobile systems for Internet access. It is not entirely clear how Mr. Obama's plan would affect zero-rated apps.

"The relevant question is whether there is something to be said about zero-rating plans and the ways that they can be used to further Internet adoption," Ms. Turner-Lee said, adding that her group had not yet taken a stance.

But critics say that zero-rating programs are just a form of paid prioritization that could further entrench companies like Facebook that have the financial muscle to pay for the privilege.

According to the Mobile Trends Charging Report by Allot Communications, nearly half of mobile broadband providers worldwide offer at least one zero-rated app, and two-thirds of those offer Facebook as one.

The alignment of civil rights groups both for and against Mr. Obama's recommendation for net-neutrality enforcement is not the only oddity in this debate.

In 2005, the Supreme Court ruled that the F.C.C. acted within the law when it classified cable broadband as a lightly regulated information service. Writing a stinging dissent to that decision — that is, saying that broadband was obviously more like a utility — was an otherwise frequent nemesis of Democrats: Justice Antonin Scalia.

F.C.C. Plans Strong Hand to Regulate the Internet

BY STEVE LOHR | FEB. 4, 2015

FOR THE LAST YEAR, Tom Wheeler, chairman of the Federal Communications Commission, has been working on new rules to ensure so-called net neutrality, or an open Internet. Over that time, his hints and comments have shown a steady shift toward stronger regulation — and a more direct confrontation with the cable television and telecommunications companies that provide high-speed Internet service to most American homes.

But on Wednesday, Mr. Wheeler went further than some industry analysts had expected and even beyond the recommendations of President Obama, who in November urged the commission to adopt the "strongest possible rules," in a surprising public admonition to an independent agency.

First, Mr. Wheeler proposed regulating consumer Internet service as a public utility, saying it was the right path to net neutrality. He also included provisions to protect consumer privacy and to ensure Internet service is available for people with disabilities and in remote areas.

Mr. Wheeler's plan would also for the first time give the F.C.C. enforcement powers to police practices in the marketplace for handling of data before it enters the gateway network into people's households — the so-called interconnect market. For good measure, he added a "future conduct" standard to cover unforeseen problems.

Some industry analysts expected Mr. Wheeler to leave some rules out of this order, partly to create a narrower target for legal challenges. Yet he chose to add the other provisions to the main thrust of his plan, which is to reclassify high-speed Internet service as a telecommunications service, instead of an information service, under Title II of the Telecommunications Act.

"Once you've decided to take the bold step — apply Title II — and open yourself up to attacks from the industry and in court, it makes sense to put in everything you want," said Kevin Werbach, a former F.C.C. counsel and an associate professor at the Wharton School of the University of Pennsylvania.

Mr. Wheeler announced the basics of his plan in an op-ed article on Wired's website Wednesday morning. Senior F.C.C. officials elaborated at a briefing later in the day.

The open Internet order, the F.C.C. officials said, will give the commission strong legal authority to ensure that no content is blocked and that the Internet is not divided into pay-to-play fast lanes for Internet and media companies that can afford it and slow lanes for everyone else. Those prohibitions are hallmarks of the net neutrality concept.

Mr. Wheeler was widely expected to take the Title II approach after President Obama urged the commission to do so. And the politics surrounding net neutrality were influenced by the nearly four million public comments the F.C.C. received last year, the vast majority urging forceful action.

Mr. Wheeler also plans to place mobile data service under the open Internet order and its Title II powers. Since the 1990s, mobile voice service has been regulated under Title II, using the light-touch model Mr. Wheeler intends to apply to broadband Internet service. That approach, for example, has shunned the regulation of pricing decisions made by cellphone operators and most business dealings between private companies to manage their mobile networks.

Mr. Wheeler has taken an ambitious step to forge a net neutrality policy, but its path ahead is anything but certain.

Mr. Wheeler will circulate his proposal to other F.C.C. commissioners on Thursday, and the plan could be modified. The proposal is subject to a vote by the full commission on Feb. 26. The commission typically decides major decisions by 3-2 votes, with the two other Democrats joining Mr. Wheeler.

If the proposal is approved, as expected, the cable and telecommunications companies have vowed to fight it in court.

"The agency is reaching for very broad powers here," said Justin Hurwitz, an assistant professor at the Nebraska College of Law. "Whether Title II applies to the Internet is very open to debate."

In Congress, Republicans are circulating draft legislation that embraces the essence of net neutrality by prohibiting content blocking and the creation of fast and slow lanes on the Internet. But their proposal would prevent the F.C.C. from issuing regulations to achieve those goals.

The opponents of utility-style rules, led by the cable and telecommunications companies, view the approach as opening a door to heavy-handed regulation that will deter investment and innovation, ultimately harming consumers.

Michael Powell, F.C.C. chairman in the Bush administration and president of the National Cable and Telecommunications Association, said in a statement that Mr. Wheeler's plan would place a "heavy burden" on broadband services and go "beyond the worthy goal of establishing important net neutrality protections."

Supporters of the Title II model include major Internet companies like Google, Facebook, Amazon and Netflix, as well as start-up companies and many public interest groups. They view the strong rules as a necessary safeguard because the Internet is increasingly the essential gateway of communication and commerce in modern life. A robust regulatory framework, they say, will ensure continued business innovation and diversity of expression.

Gene Kimmelman, president of Public Knowledge, a public advocacy group that backs Title II rules, called Mr. Wheeler's proposal a "historic initiative" to preserve an Internet system of innovation and free expression.

But Mr. Kimmelman, a former antitrust official in the Obama administration, said Mr. Wheeler's proposal represented a "natural progression" as government tries to find an appropriate regulatory framework for rapid technological change, powerful corporations and the public interest.

Net Neutrality Rules

OPINION | BY JOE NOCERA | FEB. 6, 2015

IN 2009, President Obama nominated Julius Genachowski, a trusted friend who had acted as candidate Obama's technology adviser, to be the chairman of the Federal Communications Commission. They both firmly believed in the importance of "net neutrality," in which Internet service providers, or I.S.P.s, would not be able to give one website an advantage over another, or allow companies to pay to get into a "fast lane" ahead of competitors. That was the surest way to allow innovation to flourish, they believed.

To Genachowski and his staff, creating net-neutrality protections meant reclassifying components of broadband Internet service from lightly regulated "information services" to more highly regulated "telecommunications services." This would subject I.S.P.s like Comcast and Verizon to certain "common carrier" regulations under Title II of the 1934 Communications Act. But, according to The Wall Street Journal, Larry Summers, who was then Obama's director of the National Economic Council, blocked this effort, fearful of "overly heavy-handed approaches to net neutrality" that could be detrimental to the economy.

So instead, in December 2010, the F.C.C. unveiled net-neutrality protections even while retaining the old "information services" classification. Many F.C.C. staff members knew this was a riskier approach; after all, an earlier attempt by the agency to censure Comcast for violating net-neutrality principles had been vacated by the courts — on the grounds that the F.C.C. lacked the proper authority. Sure enough, in January 2014, the court ruled that while the F.C.C. had general authority to regulate Internet traffic, it couldn't impose tougher common-carrier regulation without labeling the service providers common carriers.

Is it any wonder that Tom Wheeler, who succeeded Genachowski as chairman of the F.C.C., announced this week that he was proposing to reclassify broadband Internet services as telecommunications services? What choice did Wheeler have? "Title II is just a tool to get enforceable rules to protect end users," said Michael Beckerman, the president of the Internet Association, a trade group consisting of big Internet companies. Given the prior court decisions, that is really the only tool the government had left.

Is it truly necessary to have government-mandated rules to ensure net neutrality? Yes. One argument made by opponents of Title II classification is that we essentially have had net neutrality all along, so why does the government need to get involved? "There is no market for paid prioritization," said Berin Szoka, the president of TechFreedom, which vehemently opposes the reclassification.

But this is not necessarily because of the workings of the market. For starters, the fastest broadband providers are mostly cable companies, which are quasi monopolies. As part of its deal in buying NBCUniversal, Comcast agreed to Genachowski's net neutrality rules until 2018, regardless of the eventual court decision.

But who's to say what will happen after that? A good dose of competition might help, but other than Google Fiber — which only exists at this point in three cities — it is hard to see where that is going to come from. The way things are now, most people only have two options: their cable company or their phone company. That's not enough.

Indeed, a persuasive argument can be made that the previous attempts to create net-neutrality rules played an important role in preventing the broadband providers from, say, creating Internet fast lanes. After all, it took more than three years from the time Genachowski proposed the new net-neutrality rules to the time the court of appeals struck them down. Between those rules and the Comcast agreement, net neutrality was essentially government-mandated.

Another objection the broadband providers make is that the 1934 Communications Act is hardly the right vehicle to regulate the modern Internet. To allay these fears, Wheeler has said he would "forebear" those old regulations — such as price regulation — that don't make sense for our era. But, opponents argue, what is to prevent a future F.C.C. chairman from imposing price regulation? Surely, though, the same can be asked of the broadband providers: What is to prevent them from someday violating net neutrality if there are no rules of the road? This strikes me as by far the more credible worry.

How to classify Internet services shouldn't even be a question, and it wasn't before 2002. That's when Michael Powell, who was then the F.C.C. chairman — and is now the chief lobbyist for the cable industry — decided he wanted Internet services to be classified as an information service. He essentially commanded the F.C.C. to come up with a rationale for doing so, said Barbara Cherry, a professor at Indiana University, Bloomington, and a former F.C.C. staff member. What Wheeler is doing is not a radical step, she said. "They were classified as telecommunications services because they were telecommunications services.

"Classifying them as information services exclusively," she added, "was the real radical decision."

F.C.C. Dissenter Takes On Net Neutrality Proposal

BY STEVE LOHR | FEB. 10, 2015

THE NET NEUTRALITY talkathon got a lively and pointed contribution on Tuesday from Ajit Pai, a Republican commissioner on the Federal Communications Commission.

Mr. Pai took direct aim at the strong rules intended to preserve an open Internet, or net neutrality, that were proposed last week by Tom Wheeler, the F.C.C. chairman. Last Wednesday, Mr. Wheeler, a Democrat, rolled out the essence of his plan with an op-ed article on Wired magazine's website, followed by the distribution of a fact sheet and a lengthy briefing by senior F.C.C. officials.

On Monday, speaking at the University of Colorado, Mr. Wheeler was out on the hustings and answering critics of his approach. Under his plan, the F.C.C. would regulate broadband Internet services to American homes using a common carrier provision of the Communications Act, called Title II, whose heritage goes back to the early days of the nation's telephone network.

Mr. Wheeler said that there had been "endless repetition of the talking point" that he was proposing "old-style, 1930s monopoly regulation." He told the audience, "It's a good sound bite, but it is misleading when used to describe the modernized version of Title II that I'm proposing."

Mr. Wheeler has said repeatedly that his plan would not include regulating prices or meddling deeply in the Internet marketplace. But his approach, he insists, is needed to ensure that Internet service providers — mainly cable television and telecommunications companies — cannot block content or offer paid-for fast lanes for those who can afford it and slow lanes for those who cannot.

Mr. Pai doesn't believe that for a minute. Mr. Wheeler's plan, Mr. Pai said, would open the door to having a Washington bureaucracy "micromanage the Internet." Mr. Pai is not reassured by the proposal's pledge that the agency will refrain — or forbear, in regulatory parlance — from setting prices someday. "Expect regulation to ratchet up and forbearance to fade," he said. "The F.C.C. is going to be deciding prices."

Mr. Pai said that because the plan would permit lawsuits to challenge business practices not deemed "just and reasonable" by a plaintiff, Mr. Wheeler's proposed rules amount to "a gift to trial lawyers."

Inevitably, according to Mr. Pai, consumers will be saddled with higher costs, companies will have less incentive to invest and innovation will suffer.

In his verbal assault, Mr. Pai employed phrases original and well worn. In the latter category, he said that strong net neutrality rules are "a solution in search of a problem."

That tag line, though, suggests the substantive difference between the two camps Mr. Pai and Mr. Wheeler represent. Mr. Pai sees what he called "a very competitive marketplace" for broadband Internet service, while Mr. Wheeler's policy assumes there is not one — and thus the need for strong rules.

Much depends on how high-speed broadband is defined. The new F.C.C. standard, adopted last month, defines broadband as a download speed of 25 megabits per second or more. At that threshold, 83 percent of American households have access to high-speed broadband, but in many local markets there is only one provider at that level of service. At lower speeds, technologies like mobile broadband offer competition.

Mr. Pai called on Mr. Wheeler to publicly release the full document of his proposed order and supporting materials. Mr. Wheeler circulated his plan to the other four F.C.C. commissioners on Thursday, and they are scheduled to vote on Feb. 26. The full documents of F.C.C. proposals have not been published in the past, but Mr. Pai said this issue is of such widespread public interest that an exception should be made. Mr. Pai said he would not release it himself, adhering to commission rules.

Mr. Pai repeatedly referred to the length of the proposed order, 332 pages. But only eight of those pages are about the new rules, a senior F.C.C. official said. The rest of the document, the official said, describes how the plan would fine-tune provisions of Title II for the Internet and summarizes the four million public comments the commission received last year.

Mr. Pai also called the proposed order "President Obama's plan to regulate the Internet," a reference to Mr. Obama's public statement last November urging the commission to adopt the utility-style regulation of Title II. Taking such a public stance is unusual for a president when an independent agency is formulating policy.

Most major commission votes are split 3 to 2, with the two other Democratic commissioners joining Mr. Wheeler. Once Mr. Obama declared his position, analysts say, Mr. Wheeler pretty much had to adopt the Title II approach to get three votes on the commission.

Internet Taxes, Another Window Into the Net Neutrality Debate

BY STEVE LOHR | FEB. 20, 2015

IN A RARE ACT of bipartisan unity, Republican and Democratic senators last week presented legislation that would permanently ban taxes on high-speed Internet service to American homes.

The bipartisan moment passed quietly, and understandably so. There's no bold new step here. The legislation would make permanent a prohibition originally enacted in 1998, the Internet Tax Freedom Act, and reauthorized periodically since. The House passed a companion bill last year.

But the Senate move came shortly after Tom Wheeler, chairman of the Federal Communications Commission, proposed strong, utility-style rules to protect an open Internet, or net neutrality. That reignited the debate over whether regulation plucked from the telephone playbook, called Title II, would open the door to the imposition of state and local taxes and fees — the litany of charges on monthly phone bills.

There were echoes of different motivations in the statements last week from the two principal sponsors of the Senate bill. Ron Wyden, an Oregon Democrat and an author of the 1998 bill, emphasized the importance of the bill as a step to advance individual freedom. It was needed, Mr. Wyden said in a statement, to "protect the openness and viability of the Internet as a platform for commerce, speech, and the exchange of ideas."

The Republican sponsor, John Thune of South Dakota, emphasized economic freedom. "For 21st century innovators and entrepreneurs, the Internet is their lifeblood," Mr. Thune said. "We should be celebrating their success, not taxing the tools they use to achieve it."

JABIN BOTSFORD/THE NEW YORK TIMES

Senator John Thune of South Dakota, the Republican sponsor of legislation that would permanently ban taxes on high-speed Internet service to homes.

Mr. Thune opposes the approach being pursued by the F.C.C. chairman. The senator has prepared legislation that embraces the principles of net neutrality, including a ban on blocking web traffic or offering pay-to-play fast lanes for those who can afford it and slow lanes for everyone else. But his legislation would prohibit the F.C.C. from issuing regulations to achieve those goals.

Mr. Thune also opposes Title II regulation because he fears it could undermine the intent of the Internet tax ban. AshLee Strong, a spokeswoman for the senator, said in a statement on Thursday that net tax freedom law "eliminates a substantial amount of Internet access taxes, however it does not prohibit states and municipalities from levying new fees in a Title II world."

The Internet Tax Freedom Forever Act, according to Hal Singer, an economist and senior fellow at the Progressive Policy Institute, "limits the damage" from Title II regulation and its tax implications. Mr.

Singer is the co-author, with Robert Litan, an economist and nonresident senior fellow at the Brookings Institution, of a recent study that estimated the potential cost to consumers of Title II regulation of Internet service. (The Progressive Policy Institute's supporters include the National Cable and Telecommunications Association, which opposes Title II regulation. A spokesman for the institute, Cody Tucker, would not identify its financial backers, but he said that the research organization receives more funding from foundations, individuals and corporations that support Title II classification for broadband Internet service than oppose it.)

The potential pitfall, Mr. Singer said, is that the Internet tax freedom law mainly bans "general sales taxes," but there is still room for states and municipalities to assess fees that are related to the "obligations of a telecommunications provider." In their study, the two economists assembled a database of the taxes and fees states place on phone bills, and then assumed those charges would be levied proportionately on Internet broadband service.

State practices vary, but if you add them all up and assume the worst, the study forecast the additional costs to the nation's consumers would be $15 billion a year. The Internet tax freedom act would bring that worst-case estimate down to $11 billion, as they calculated in the follow-up blog post.

The F.C.C. staff says this kind of analysis is off-base, raising unjustified fears. Mr. Wheeler's plan, Kim Hart, a spokeswoman for the F.C.C., said, "does not raise taxes or fees. Period." And, she added, the Internet tax freedom act "bans state and local taxes on broadband access regardless of how the F.C.C. classifies it."

The fault line on the tax issue, as in so much of the debate surrounding Mr. Wheeler's plan, hinges on how open-ended or how restrained his tailored model of Title II regulation of Internet service is likely to be.

F.C.C. Approves Net Neutrality Rules, Classifying Broadband Internet Service as a Utility

BY REBECCA R. RUIZ AND STEVE LOHR | FEB. 26, 2015

WASHINGTON — The Federal Communications Commission voted on Thursday to regulate broadband Internet service as a public utility, a milestone in regulating high-speed Internet service into American homes.

Tom Wheeler, the commission chairman, said the F.C.C. was using "all the tools in our toolbox to protect innovators and consumers" and preserve the Internet's role as a "core of free expression and democratic principles."

The new rules, approved 3 to 2 along party lines, are intended to ensure that no content is blocked and that the Internet is not divided into pay-to-play fast lanes for Internet and media companies that can afford it and slow lanes for everyone else. Those prohibitions are hallmarks of the net neutrality concept.

Explaining the reason for the regulation, Mr. Wheeler, a Democrat, said that Internet access was "too important to let broadband providers be the ones making the rules."

Mobile data service for smartphones and tablets, in addition to wired lines, is being placed under the new rules. The order also includes provisions to protect consumer privacy and to ensure that Internet service is available to people with disabilities and in remote areas.

Before the vote, each of the five commissioners spoke and the Republicans delivered a scathing critique of the order as overly broad, vague and unnecessary. Ajit Pai, a Republican commissioner, said the rules were government meddling in a vibrant, competitive market and were likely to deter investment, undermine innovation and ultimately harm consumers.

"The Internet is not broken," Mr. Pai said. "There is no problem to solve."

The impact of the new rules will hinge partly on details that are not yet known. The rules will not be published for at least a couple of days, and will not take effect for probably at least a couple of months. Lawsuits to challenge the commission's order are widely expected.

The F.C.C. is taking this big regulatory step by reclassifying high-speed Internet service as a telecommunications service, instead of an information service, under Title II of the Telecommunications Act. The Title II classification comes from the phone company era, treating service as a public utility.

But the new rules are an à la carte version of Title II, adopting some provisions and shunning others. The F.C.C. will not get involved in pricing decisions or the engineering decisions companies make in managing their networks. Mr. Wheeler, who gave a forceful defense of the rules just ahead of the vote, said the tailored approach was anything but old-style utility regulation. "These are a 21st-century set of rules for a 21st-century industry," he said.

Opponents of the new rules, led by cable television and telecommunications companies, say adopting the Title II approach opens the door to bureaucratic interference with business decisions that, if let stand, would reduce incentives to invest and thus raise prices and hurt consumers.

"Today, the F.C.C. took one of the most regulatory steps in its history," Michael Powell, president of the National Cable and Telecommunications Association and a chairman of the F.C.C. in the Bush administration, said in a statement. "The commission has breathed new life into the decayed telephone regulatory model and applied it to the most dynamic, freewheeling and innovative platform in history."

Supporters of the Title II model include many major Internet companies, start-ups and public interest groups. In a statement, Michael Beckerman, president of the Internet Association, which includes Google, Facebook and smaller online companies, called the F.C.C.

vote "a welcome step in our effort to create strong, enforceable net neutrality rules."

The F.C.C.'s yearlong path to issuing rules to ensure an open Internet precipitated an extraordinary level of political involvement, from grass-roots populism to the White House, for a regulatory ruling. The F.C.C. received four million comments, about a quarter of them generated through a campaign organized by groups including Fight for the Future, an advocacy nonprofit.

Evan Greer, campaign director for Fight for the Future, said, "This shows that the Internet has changed the rules of what can be accomplished in Washington."

An overwhelming majority of the comments supported common-carrier style rules, like those in the order the commission approved on Thursday.

In the public meeting, Mr. Wheeler began his remarks by noting the flood of public comments. "We listened and we learned," he said.

GABRIELLA DEMCZUK FOR THE NEW YORK TIMES

Supporters of net neutrality rallied on Thursday outside the F.C.C. building.

In November, President Obama took the unusual step of urging the F.C.C., an independent agency, to adopt the "strongest possible rules" on net neutrality.

Mr. Obama specifically called on the commission to classify high-speed broadband service as a utility under Title II. His rationale: "For most Americans, the Internet has become an essential part of everyday communication and everyday life."

Republicans in Congress were slow to react, and initially misread the public mood. Senator Ted Cruz of Texas portrayed the F.C.C. rule-making process as a heavy-handed liberal initiative, "Obamacare for the Internet."

In January, Senator John Thune, the South Dakota Republican, began circulating legislation that embraced the principles of net neutrality, banning both paid-for priority lanes and the blocking or throttling of any web content. But it would also prohibit the F.C.C. from issuing regulations to achieve those goals. This week, the Republicans pulled back, with too little support to move quickly.

Also at the Thursday meeting, the F.C.C. approved an order to preempt state laws that limit the build-out of municipal broadband Internet services. The order focuses on laws in two states, North Carolina and Tennessee, but it would create a policy framework for other states. About 20 states, by the F.C.C.'s count, have laws that restrict the activities of community broadband services.

The state laws unfairly restrict municipal competition with cable and telecommunications broadband providers, the F.C.C. said. This order, too, will surely be challenged in court.

REBECCA R. RUIZ REPORTED FROM WASHINGTON, AND STEVE LOHR FROM NEW YORK.

Reaction to Regulation: 1934 vs. Today

BY REBECCA R. RUIZ | MARCH 5, 2015

LAST WEEK, the Federal Communications Commission voted to regulate Internet service as a public utility, reclassifying broadband providers under Title II of the Communications Act of 1934 and subjecting them to stricter rules. Republicans and many broadband providers have criticized the decision, arguing that it was driven by the president and gives the federal government too much control, draws on dated laws and will result in subjective interpretations of broad mandates.

Sure sounds familiar.

Eight decades ago, when Congress passed the Communications Act of 1934 and created the F.C.C., Republican lawmakers objected just as loudly, and with similar concerns.

Two senators — Lester J. Dickinson, Republican of Iowa, and Thomas D. Schall, Republican of Minnesota — strongly opposed the 1934 legislation. They called President Franklin D. Roosevelt's administration "desperate" and overreaching. The senators said the act was an attempt to "censor the press" by seeking to regulate telegraph companies and broaden the Radio Act of 1927, according to news coverage at the time from The New York Times.

In February 1934, President Roosevelt had asked Congress to create the F.C.C. to centralize authority over radio, telephone and telegraph services. On Feb. 26 of that year, The Times, on its front page, reported the recommendations made by the president and a committee he had created to study electronic communications:

The committee's study led it to believe that rates for the various services could be lowered through regulation of company profits, overhead expenses and intercompany charges.

The committee felt, further, that a single independent government agency could prevent discrimination, regulation of annual depreciation charges and extension of service to localities and homes not now served.

By June, legislation along the lines of President Roosevelt's vision passed both the House and Senate and was signed into law by the president on June 19. But leading up to that, The Times reported on strong Republican dissent.

On March 18, 1934, the paper quoted Senator Dickinson of Iowa as saying: "Only a united front by the press of the nation can halt this new plan to gag them. The newspapers of the United States must prevent the fourth attempt to Hitlerize the press of the nation."

Senator Schall of Minnesota spoke similarly, calling the F.C.C. bill for telegraph and wireless companies a "national libel law." As The Times wrote:

> *He asserted the bill established the proposed commission as a censorship agency and that the result of the bill would be the holding up of press dispatches until "a censor from the Federal Communications Commission passes on the subject-matter."*

He added: "Of course, since it is necessary for a telegraph company to secure a license from this commission before it can operate, this in itself, since the license is revocable, is censorship in every sense of the word."

Still, when the law took effect on July 1, 1934, reaction was more moderately characterized in The Times. As a story published on that date read, "Leaders Foresee No Material Shifts in Broadcasting — Much Depends Upon Personnel of Commission." It speculated that the impact of the new act would depend on whether there was a Democratic or Republican majority.

That same sentiment was expressed repeatedly last week, with lawmakers and nonpartisan experts alike wondering how enforcement of some new rules might change based on which party holds the majority.

As Louis G. Caldwell, former general counsel of the F.C.C., told The Times in July 1934 about the communications act: "Regulation under the new law will be as good or as bad as the personnel."

Today, as the public awaits the release of the full text of the new 2015 rules that will govern broadband Internet service, similar concerns are being raised.

Testifying before a House subcommittee last week about F.C.C.'s vote, Robert D. Atkinson, founder and president of the Information Technology and Innovation Foundation, a technology policy organization, warned of changed policies under changing leadership. "It's unclear how future commissions will treat this authority," he said. "One of the most vibrant sectors of our economy becomes unpredictable from one administration to the next."

Congress Scrutinizes F.C.C. Following Release of New Internet Rules

BY REBECCA R. RUIZ | MARCH 17, 2015

NEARLY THREE WEEKS after the Federal Communications Commission voted to regulate broadband Internet like a public utility, Congress is putting the agency and its new rules under the microscope.

On Tuesday, in the first of five Congressional hearings on the agency in the next two weeks, Republican members of the House Committee on Oversight & Government Reform raised questions about whether the White House improperly influenced the F.C.C., an independent agency. In a public video last fall, President Obama urged the agency to pass strong regulation. On Thursday, the F.C.C. released the full text of its new rules, which fall under Title II of the Communications Act and are intended to protect the open Internet by prohibiting service providers from speeding up or slowing down users' access to certain kinds of content.

Facing a tough tone from Republican lawmakers about his handling of the rules, Tom Wheeler, chairman of the F.C.C., pushed back repeatedly, arguing that the president had no undue influence on his rule-making.

Mr. Wheeler, a former top fund-raiser for Mr. Obama, said that the president had not seen the text of the controversial order prior to the agency's vote on it last month. He added that he had been in the Oval Office only once since he became chairman, days after he was appointed in November 2013.

"In that meeting, he said, 'I will never call you. You are an independent agency,' " Mr. Wheeler said of Mr. Obama. "And he has been good to his word."

Republicans focused on 10 meetings Mr. Wheeler had with various members of the White House over the last year, asking about the substance of each conversation. Mr. Wheeler said that many of those meetings had focused on unrelated issues, including trade, hacking and the agency's auction of new airwaves for wireless broadband.

And Rep. Jason Chaffetz, a Republican from Utah and chairman of the committee, announced that the Inspector General of the F.C.C. was undertaking an investigation into how the agency arrived at its rules, an inquiry that Mr. Wheeler said he did not know about.

Questions from elected representatives had a tone of interrogation that Peter Welch, Democratic representative from Vermont, called reminiscent of the Watergate hearings for their fixation on "what did you know and when did you know it," regarding Mr. Wheeler's digestion of President Obama's input.

Rep. John Mica, a Republican from Florida, said he thought it was clear that Mr. Wheeler had been "strong armed" into a position vastly different than the one he had originally held.

Democratic lawmakers, meanwhile, argued that the actions of the White House were consistent with actions of previous administrations. Some Democrats pointed out that presidents including Ronald Reagan, George H.W. Bush and Bill Clinton had expressed their opinions to the F.C.C., too.

"The president was not and should not have been silenced," said Eleanor Holmes Norton, a Democrat from the District of Columbia.

Mr. Wheeler emphasized both his agency's independence and its natural consideration of a variety of perspectives — those voiced by members of Congress, by the millions of members of the public who submitted comments on the issue, and by the president. He added that the F.C.C.'s rules were not entirely reflective of Mr. Obama's specific vision.

Mr. Chaffetz, the Republican committee chairman, criticized not the rules themselves but the agency's process of passing and releasing them. He took particular issue with the two weeks between when the agency voted on the new rules and published them.

The rules were subject to a period of so-called editorial privilege, typical of the F.C.C.'s rule-making process, that allows the agency to make non-substantive final edits after a vote, in order to address dissenting arguments and legal questions to better protect against court challenges. The delayed release of the new rules was not unusual; past chairmen of the agency have, on occasion, taken several months to release the full text of an order.

Four similar hearings with lawmakers are scheduled within the next two weeks, including ones called by the Senate Commerce Committee and the House Judiciary Committee. The tone of each is expected to be similarly sharp and divided along party lines.

But as Mr. Wheeler anticipates further scrutiny, he said he remained confident in and proud of the agency's choices. "There is no way I am apologetic," he said. "I am fiercely proud of this decision."

How Netflix Keeps Finding Itself on the Same Side as Regulators

BY JAMES B. STEWART | MAY 28, 2015

WHATEVER THE OUTCOME of the latest proposed mergers and acquisitions in the media industry, a clear winner has already emerged, and it's not even a party to any of the deals: Netflix, the streaming television pioneer.

To many in the cable and broadband businesses, the invisible hand of Netflix has been apparent in the failed Comcast-Time Warner Cable combination; in likely restrictions on the merger between AT&T and DirecTV; and in the Obama administration's embrace of net neutrality, to cite just three prominent examples.

Indeed, the corporate philosophy of Netflix, which was once thought to be outgunned in Washington by the East Coast media conglomerates and their vast lobbying forces, now seems so pervasive that the Federal Communications Commission, or F.C.C., is being referred to by some media executives — half-jokingly and half-enviously — as the "N.C.C."

But Netflix is hardly the only corporate beneficiary. To varying degrees, an array of Silicon Valley powerhouses — including Google, Amazon, Facebook and Apple — gain from an open Internet and net neutrality, the notion that broadband service providers should treat all data equally, no matter its content, source or volume. That these views have prevailed over long-entrenched telecommunication and cable interests is yet further evidence of the technology industry's growing political clout inside the White House and on Capitol Hill.

Netflix hasn't yet taken a position on Charter Communications' $67.1 billion purchases of Time Warner Cable and Bright House Networks, which were announced this week. But if Charter's chief executive, Thomas M. Rutledge, wants to avoid the fate of Brian Roberts, Comcast's chairman, he'd better get on the phone with Netflix's chief executive, Reed Hastings, before it's too late.

"Netflix has raised some very legitimate issues, and they've done an excellent job of presenting their vision of the market," said Gene Kimmelman, who dealt with Netflix while he was chief counsel at the antitrust division and now runs Public Knowledge, which supports an open Internet.

At the same time, he said, the influence of any one voice shouldn't be exaggerated. "Their story just happened to fit perfectly into a broader narrative of the potential for harm to consumers," Mr. Kimmelman said. But "Netflix's role is definitely an important piece of the puzzle."

From Netflix's point of view, the fact that its views have gained traction with regulators is merely a recognition that its corporate philosophy, which it says has always been to put consumer interests first, coincides with sound public policy. It has opposed mergers like Comcast-Time Warner Cable and sought conditions in others that it feels pose a threat to broadband competition and innovation and to an open Internet.

"These broadband issues galvanized many — more than four million Americans, various companies and consumers groups — who all stressed the importance of a free and open Internet," Corie Wright, director of public policy at Netflix, which is based in Los Gatos, Calif., told me this week. "To the extent the F.C.C. and Justice Department's decisions reflect a strong focus on Internet consumers, that's an encouraging sign of good policy-making."

Netflix points out that its competitors also benefit from an unfettered Internet. So do other streaming services like Hulu and Amazon, as well as industry stalwarts like HBO and CBS that have started their own so-called over-the-top offerings. Verizon, which this month struck a deal to buy AOL, is also poised to introduce its own Internet television offering.

But Netflix, for better or worse, has become the symbol for net neutrality, which has become a key issue in how regulators analyze proposed cable and telecom mergers.

Of course, government antitrust and communications policy is supposed to benefit consumers, not any individual company or group of companies. "It's fair to say Netflix has gotten something of a free pass," said Scott Hemphill, visiting professor of antitrust and intellectual property at New York University School of Law. "This open Internet principle that's in ascendance is certainly good for Netflix. It's harder to say it's good for consumers."

A pivotal moment in the net neutrality struggle came last year when Netflix agreed to pay Comcast so-called interconnection fees, a deal that Netflix's Mr. Hastings last month called a "deal with the devil." (While Comcast has drawn the brunt of Mr. Hastings's ire, Netflix also reached similar interconnection deals with every other major Internet service provider.)

But securing payment from Netflix for fast and more reliable access may have been a Pyrrhic victory for Comcast and the other the broadband providers. Until then the notion of net neutrality had been something of an abstraction. But when Netflix subscribers found their programs constantly interrupted for "buffering" (an interruption to download more data), the ability of Internet providers to play favorites seemed all too real. Once Netflix started paying fees to Comcast, its customers suddenly found their service improved substantially.

A Comcast spokeswoman declined to comment. But Comcast has offered a different narrative, asserting that Cogent Communications, an intermediary that lacked adequate data capacity, caused Netflix's problems. Once Netflix paid Comcast's interconnection fee and connected directly to Comcast's network, the bottleneck largely vanished.

Still, Netflix's experience with Comcast became Exhibit A with the F.C.C. when Netflix opposed the proposed Comcast-Time Warner Cable merger. "The combined company would possess even more anti-competitive leverage to charge arbitrary interconnection tolls for access to their customers," Netflix said in a letter to shareholders opposing the merger.

It probably didn't hurt Netflix's case that just about everyone in Washington watches the hit Netflix series "House of Cards," and Comcast is the dominant Internet provider there. Tom Wheeler, the F.C.C.

chairman, said he, too, had suffered buffering problems, which he called "exasperating."

Mr. Wheeler didn't mention Netflix in his statement last month praising Comcast's decision to abandon its bid for Time Warner Cable, which he called "in the best interests of consumers." But he echoed Netflix's position in calling the merger an "unacceptable risk to competition and innovation" given "the growing importance of high-speed broadband to online video and innovative new services."

Despite Netflix's arguments that it shouldn't have to pay fees to a broadband provider, that proposition is hardly self-evident. The fees Netflix so fiercely opposes are analogous to those found in many industries, such as credit cards, where both consumers and merchants pay the credit card companies. "It's hard to say if these fees are good or bad for consumers," Professor Hemphill said.

But Netflix has aggressively pushed the argument that interconnection fees are different because the gatekeepers have too much power and an incentive to abuse it. If regulators continue to sympathize with Netflix's position, AT&T may have to make at least some of the concessions in its proposed $48 billion takeover of DirecTV. Netflix isn't opposing the merger outright, but in a letter this month, and in meetings with F.C.C. officials, it has raised concerns similar to those in the Comcast merger: that a combined AT&T-DirecTV has an incentive to protect its existing cable program bundles by imposing data caps or usage fees that disadvantage Netflix and other streaming services using its broadband network.

And now there's Charter's proposed acquisition of Time Warner Cable. Even if Netflix doesn't come out as forcefully against the merger as it did with the Comcast deal, its position will surely reverberate during the government's review.

This week, Charter seemed already to be anticipating Netflix's likely objections and pledged fealty to the notion of net neutrality. "We have no plans to block, throttle or engage in paid prioritization because our customers demand an open Internet," Mr. Rutledge said in a conference call announcing the deal.

But if regulators apply the same reasoning they appeared to have used in analyzing the Comcast bid, that may not be enough.

It's true that a combined Charter-Time Warner Cable wouldn't be nearly as large, giving it about 30 percent of the high-speed broadband market, nor does it own a content provider like NBCUniversal. But viewed as a national market, Internet service is already highly concentrated, with only a few major competitors. Arguing the proposition that combining three of them into one is in consumers' interest may be tough given that the Obama administration has publicly complained about the lack of broadband competition.

Senator Al Franken, the Minnesota Democrat who strongly opposed the Comcast deal, has already sent letters to the Justice Department and F.C.C. saying, "Any deal of this size and scope warrants scrutiny."

Court Backs Rules Treating Internet as Utility, Not Luxury

BY CECILIA KANG | JUNE 14, 2016

WASHINGTON — High-speed internet service can be defined as a utility, a federal court has ruled in a sweeping decision clearing the way for more rigorous policing of broadband providers and greater protections for web users.

The decision affirmed the government's view that broadband is as essential as the phone and power and should be available to all Americans, rather than a luxury that does not need close government supervision.

The 2-to-1 decision from a three-judge panel at the United States Court of Appeals for the District of Columbia Circuit on Tuesday came in a case about rules applying to a doctrine known as net neutrality, which prohibit broadband companies from blocking or slowing the delivery of internet content to consumers.

Those rules, created by the Federal Communications Commission in early 2015, started a huge legal battle as cable, telecom and wireless internet providers sued to overturn regulations that they said went far beyond the F.C.C.'s authority and would hurt their businesses. On the other side, millions of consumers and giant tech firms rallied in favor of the regulations. President Obama also called for the strictest possible mandates on broadband providers.

The court's decision upheld the F.C.C. on the declaration of broadband as a utility, which was the most significant aspect of the rules. That has broad-reaching implications for web and telecommunications companies that have battled for nearly a decade over the need for regulation to ensure web users get full and equal access to all content online.

"After a decade of debate and legal battles, today's ruling affirms the commission's ability to enforce the strongest possible internet protections — both on fixed and mobile networks — that will ensure the internet remains open, now and in the future," Tom Wheeler, chairman of the F.C.C., said in a statement.

The two judges who ruled in favor of the F.C.C. emphasized the importance of the internet as an essential communications and information platform for consumers.

"Over the past two decades, this content has transformed nearly every aspect of our lives, from profound actions like choosing a leader, building a career, and falling in love to more quotidian ones like hailing a cab and watching a movie," wrote David Tatel and Sri Srinivasan, the judges who wrote the opinion.

But the legal battle over the regulations is most likely far from over. The cable and telecom industries have signaled their intent to challenge any unfavorable decision, possibly taking the case to the Supreme Court.

AT&T immediately said it would continue to fight.

"We have always expected this issue to be decided by the Supreme Court and we look forward to participating in that appeal," said David McAtee II, the senior executive vice president and general counsel for AT&T.

For now, the decision limits the ability of broadband providers like Comcast and Verizon to shape the experience of internet users. Without net neutrality rules, the broadband providers could be inclined to deliver certain content on the web at slower speeds, for example, making the streams on Netflix or YouTube buffer or shut down. Such business decisions by broadband providers would have created fast and slow lanes on the internet, subjecting businesses and consumers to extra charges and limited access to content online, the F.C.C. has argued.

"This is an enormous win for consumers," said Gene Kimmelman, president of the public interest group Public Knowledge. "It ensures the right to an open internet with no gatekeepers."

The 184-page ruling also opens a path for new limits on broadband providers beyond net neutrality. Already, the F.C.C. has proposed privacy rules for broadband providers, curbing the ability of companies like Verizon and AT&T to collect and share data about broadband subscribers.

Google and Netflix support net neutrality rules and have warned government officials that without regulatory limits, broadband providers will have an incentive to create business models that could harm consumers. They argue that broadband providers could degrade the quality of downloads and streams of online services to extract tolls from web companies or to promote unfairly their own competing services or the content of partners.

The court's ruling was a certainty for the F.C.C. Two of the three judges who heard the case late last year agreed that wireless broadband services were also common carrier utility services that were subject to anti-blocking and discrimination rules, a decision protested by wireless carriers including AT&T and Verizon Wireless.

In the opinion, the two judges in favor of the rules said internet users don't feel the difference between fixed-wire broadband and mobile service. To an iPad user, whose device switches automatically between Wi-Fi and wireless networks, the government's oversight of those technologies should not differ, they said.

Tech firms cheered the decision, which they said would be particularly helpful to start-ups that did not have the resources to fight gatekeepers of the web.

"Today marks a huge victory for the millions of microbusinesses who depend on the open internet to reach consumers and compete in the global marketplace," said Althea Erickson, the senior director of global policy at the online crafts marketplace Etsy.

In a statement, the cable industry's biggest lobbying group highlighted the comments of the dissenting judge, Stephen Williams, and said that its members were reviewing the opinion. The group also said broadband legislation by Congress was a better alternative to the F.C.C.'s classification of internet business as a utility.

"While this is unlikely the last step in this decade-long debate over internet regulation, we urge bipartisan leaders in Congress to renew their efforts to craft meaningful legislation that can end ongoing uncertainty, promote network investment and protect consumers," the National Cable and Telecommunications Association said in a statement.

In his lengthy dissenting opinion, Mr. Williams called the rules an "unreasoned patchwork" that will discourage competition in the broadband industry.

The biggest threat to broadband providers is the potential of any regulations to hurt the rates they charge for the service, analysts said. The F.C.C. has promised it will not impose rate regulations on the firms like it does for phone companies.

"The pendulum has today swung a bit further in the direction of long-term price regulation," said Craig Moffett, an analyst at the research firm MoffettNathanson.

The F.C.C. was divided along party lines on the rules. It began its quest for net neutrality rules in 2009, with two previous attempts at creating rules overturned by the same court.

In a statement, Ajit Pai, a Republican commissioner who was among a minority who opposed the regulation of broadband as a utility, urged cable and telecom firms to keep going with their legal challenge.

"I continue to believe that these regulations are unlawful, and I hope that the parties challenging them will continue the legal fight," he said.

CHAPTER 4

Repeal, Protest and the Uncertain Future of Net Neutrality

In January 2017, following the resignation of Tom Wheeler from the post, President Donald J. Trump appointed Ajit Pai as the new chair of the Federal Communications Commission. As a minority Republican member of the F.C.C., Pai had voted against the Open Internet Order and often criticized the F.C.C.'s strong regulatory role. In December 2017, the F.C.C. voted to roll back net neutrality. In response, state attorney generals, state legislatures, members of Congress, and activists fought back with protests, legislation, and lawsuits.

Trump's F.C.C. Pick Quickly Targets Net Neutrality Rules

BY CECILIA KANG | FEB. 5, 2017

WASHINGTON — In his first days as President Trump's pick to lead the Federal Communications Commission, Ajit Pai has aggressively moved to roll back consumer protection regulations created during the Obama presidency.

Mr. Pai took a first swipe at net neutrality rules designed to ensure equal access to content on the internet. He stopped nine companies from providing discounted high-speed internet service to low-income individuals. He withdrew an effort to keep prison phone rates down, and he scrapped a proposal to break open the cable box market.

In total, as the chairman of the F.C.C., Mr. Pai released about a dozen actions in the last week, many buried in the agency's website and not publicly announced, stunning consumer advocacy groups and telecom analysts. They said Mr. Pai's message was clear: The F.C.C., an independent agency, will mirror the Trump administration's rapid unwinding of government regulations that businesses fought against during the Obama administration.

"With these strong-arm tactics, Chairman Pai is showing his true stripes," said Matt Wood, the policy director at the consumer group Free Press.

"The public wants an F.C.C. that helps people," he added. "Instead, it got one that does favors for the powerful corporations that its chairman used to work for."

Mr. Pai, a former lawyer for Verizon, was elevated by Mr. Trump to the position of chairman after serving as a minority Republican member for the past three years. Known for being a stickler on conservative interpretations of telecommunications law and the limits of the F.C.C.'s authority, Mr. Pai said he was trying to wipe the slate clean.

He noted that his predecessor, Tom Wheeler, had rammed through a series of actions right after the presidential election. Many of those efforts, Mr. Pai argued, went beyond the agency's legal authority.

"These last-minute actions, which did not enjoy the support of the majority of commissioners at the time they were taken, should not bind us going forward," Mr. Pai said in a statement released Friday. "Accordingly, they are being revoked."

The efforts portend great changes at the federal agency at the center of the convergence of media, telecommunications and the internet. The biggest target will be net neutrality, a rule created in 2015 that prevents internet service providers from blocking or discriminating against internet traffic. The rule, which was created alongside a

ERIC THAYER FOR THE NEW YORK TIMES

Ajit Pai, the Federal Communications Commission chairman.

decision to categorize broadband like a utility, was the tech centerpiece of the Obama administration.

On Friday, the F.C.C. took its first steps to pull back those rules, analysts said. Mr. Pai closed an investigation into zero-rating practices of the wireless providers T-Mobile, AT&T and Verizon. Zero-rating is the offering of free streaming and other downloads that do not count against limits on the amount of data a consumer can download.

If a provider like AT&T offers free streaming of its DirecTV programs, does that violate net neutrality rules because it could put competing video services at a disadvantage? Under its previous leadership, the F.C.C. said in a report that it saw some evidence that made it concerned. But Mr. Pai said after closing the investigations into wireless carriers that zero-rating was popular among consumers, particularly low-income households.

"The speed of the ruling and the chairman's tone are very encouraging for internet service providers," said Paul Gallant, an analyst at

Cowen. "I think it's a down payment on net neutrality, with much more to follow."

Last week, Mr. Pai said he disagreed with the move two years ago to declare broadband a utility. The reclassification of broadband into a service akin to telephones and electricity provided the legal foundation for net neutrality rules.

Mr. Pai said he had not decided how he would approach the overhaul of broadband classification and net neutrality rules, but he faces legal hurdles. A federal court upheld the rules last year, and the commission could end up in a lengthy legal battle if he tries to scrap the rules.

Mr. Pai will have the help of powerful members of Congress who have promised to attack the classification of broadband as a utility-like service. And he is popular among Republican leaders, including the Senate's majority leader, Mitch McConnell, who with other members viewed Mr. Pai as a loyal voice of dissent during the Obama years. Mr. Pai, 44, the child of immigrants from India who settled in Kansas, is a fresh face for the Republican Party.

Congress could introduce legislation that limits the agency's ability to regulate broadband providers and enforce net neutrality rules. Also under attack are privacy rules for broadband providers.

"The agency has strayed from its core mission," said Marsha Blackburn, a Republican representative from Tennessee who oversees a telecommunications and tech subcommittee. She has called for a hearing within two weeks on the F.C.C. agenda under the new administration.

Democrats in Congress said they would fight legislation that waters down net neutrality rules. They said Mr. Pai, described as a straight-A student of telecom law, would be a tough adversary, and they face great opposition from Republicans who have promised to prioritize the overturning of net neutrality rules.

"The key here is that it's already been tested in the courts and the court upheld this," said Representative Anna G. Eshoo, Democrat of

California. "Ajit Pai is intelligent and genial, but he is not on the side of consumers and the public interest."

Most troubling to consumer advocates was the secrecy around Mr. Pai's early actions. That included a decision to rescind the permissions of nine broadband providers to participate in a federal subsidy plan for low-income consumers. None of the providers currently serve low-income consumers, but Mr. Pai's comments could foreshadow a shake-up of the Lifeline low-income subsidy program.

On Monday, the F.C.C. is scheduled to appear before a federal judge to defend its push to curb extraordinarily expensive phone call prices from prison. But it told a judge a few days ago that Mr. Pai disagreed with many aspects of the case.

Mignon Clyburn, the sole Democrat of the three sitting members of the F.C.C., warned that the actions would directly harm consumers. "Rather than working to close the digital divide, this action widens the gap," Ms. Clyburn said.

F.C.C. Chairman Pushes Sweeping Changes to Net Neutrality Rules

BY CECILIA KANG | APRIL 26, 2017

WASHINGTON — The chairman of the Federal Communications Commission on Wednesday outlined a sweeping plan to loosen the government's oversight of high-speed internet providers, a rebuke of a landmark policy approved two years ago to ensure that all online content is treated the same by the companies that deliver broadband service to Americans.

The chairman, Ajit Pai, said high-speed internet service should no longer be treated like a public utility with strict rules, as it is now. The move would, in effect, largely leave the industry to police itself.

The plan is Mr. Pai's most forceful action in his race to roll back rules that govern telecommunications, cable and broadcasting companies, which he says are harmful to business. But he is certain to face a contentious battle with the consumers and tech companies that rallied around the existing rules, which are meant to prevent broadband providers like AT&T and Comcast from giving special treatment to any streaming videos, news sites and other content.

"Two years ago, I warned that we were making a serious mistake," Mr. Pai said at the Newseum in Washington, where he laid out the plan in a speech. "It's basic economics. The more heavily you regulate something, the less of it you're likely to get."

His plan, though still vague on the details, is a sharp change from the approach taken by the last F.C.C. administration, which approved rules governing a concept known as net neutrality in 2015. The rules were intended to ensure an open internet, meaning that no content could be blocked by broadband providers and that the internet would not be divided into pay-to-play fast lanes for internet and media companies that can afford it and slow lanes for everyone else.

The policy was the signature telecom regulation of the Obama era. It classified broadband as a common carrier service akin to phones, which are subject to strong government oversight. President Obama made an unusual public push for the reclassification in a video message that was widely shared and appeared to embolden the last F.C.C. chairman, Tom Wheeler, to make the change.

The classification also led to the creation of broadband privacy rules in 2016 that made it harder to collect and sell browsing information and other user data. Last month, President Trump signed a bill overturning the broadband privacy regulations, which would have gone into effect at the end of the year.

In his speech on Wednesday, Mr. Pai said he would undo that classification.

Mr. Pai said he was generally supportive of the idea behind net neutrality but said the rules went too far and were not necessary for an open internet. He said he would also seek public comment on how to preserve the basic principles of net neutrality — the prohibitions of blocking, throttling and paid priority for online traffic.

Mr. Pai voted against the current rules as a commissioner. Critics of his ideas for changing the rules warned that making any commitments only voluntary would pave the way for the creation of business practices that harm competition.

"It would put consumers at the mercy of phone and cable companies," said Craig Aaron, president of the consumer advocacy group Free Press. "In a fantasy world, all would be fine with a pinkie swear not to interrupt pathways and portals to the internet despite a history of doing that."

The new policy faces several hurdles before going into effect, including months of comments and revisions. But Republicans have a 2 to 1 majority on the commission, including Mr. Pai, so most proposals he puts up for a vote will generally be expected to pass.

Consumer groups and tech companies have warned of a legal challenge, however. The current net neutrality rules were affirmed by a federal appeals court, which could put an extra burden on Mr. Pai to justify his changes.

Last week, Mr. Pai went to Silicon Valley to meet with executives of tech companies like Facebook, Oracle, Cisco and Intel to solicit their support for revisions to the broadband rules. The Silicon Valley companies are divided on their views about the existing policy, with internet companies like Facebook supporting strong rules and hardware and chip makers open to Mr. Pai's changes.

The F.C.C.'s policing of broadband companies has drawn greater interest with recent proposals for big mergers, such as AT&T's $85 billion bid for Time Warner, that create huge media conglomerates that distribute and own video content. Already, AT&T is giving mobile subscribers free streaming access to television content by DirecTV, which it owns. Consumer groups have complained that such practices, known as sponsored data, put rivals at a disadvantage and could help determine what news and information is most likely to reach consumers.

Telecom and cable companies applauded the announcement on Wednesday. Since Mr. Pai's appointment in January by President Trump, their lobbyists have flooded the agency and the offices of Congress, pushing for an unwinding of rules that they say hamper their businesses. The No. 1 target has been the rules on broadband providers, which they complain have crimped their willingness to invest in their networks.

"We applaud F.C.C. Chairman Pai's initiative to remove this stifling regulatory cloud over the internet," Randall L. Stephenson, AT&T's chief executive, said in a statement. "It was illogical for the F.C.C. in 2015 to abandon that light-touch approach and instead regulate the internet under an 80-year-old law designed to set rates for the rotary-dial-telephone era."

Mr. Pai has been an active figure in the Trump administration's quest to dismantle regulations. He froze a broadband subsidy program for low-income households, eased limits on television station mergers and eased caps on how much a company like AT&T or Comcast can charge another business to get online.

Consumer groups have opposed some of his changes, and they challenged the assertions of telecom companies that broadband regulations harm their businesses. They said publicly traded broadband companies have increased investments in their networks 5 percent since the current rules went into effect.

About 800 tech start-ups and investors, organized by the Silicon Valley incubator Y Combinator and the San Francisco policy advocacy group Engine, protested the unwinding of net neutrality in a letter sent to Mr. Pai on Wednesday.

"Without net neutrality, the incumbents who provide access to the internet would be able to pick winners or losers in the market," they wrote in the letter.

So far, Google and Netflix, the most vocal proponents of net neutrality in previous years, have not spoken individually about Mr. Pai's proposal. Speaking through their trade group, the Internet Association, they said the broadband and net neutrality rules should stay intact.

"Rolling back these rules or reducing the legal sustainability of the order will result in a worse internet for consumers and less innovation online," Michael Beckerman, chief executive of the Internet Association, said in a statement.

Mr. Pai vowed a strong commitment to the plan: "Make no mistake about it: This is a fight that we intend to wage and it is a fight that we are going to win."

Net Neutrality: Why Artists and Activists Can't Afford to Lose It

OPINION | BY W. KAMAU BELL | OCT. 31, 2017

SOMEWHERE at a comedy club, a new comedian is about to hit the stage for the first time. She will bring with her the modern tool of the trade: her cellphone, equipped with the notes she has typed, a recording app, and five minutes of material that isn't worth all that technology. This set is going to bomb. Hard. But she will repeat this process — night in, night out, until over time, that five-minute performance becomes tighter and more polished. Eventually, she'll ask a friend to use a phone to record a set. And that night she will kill. Utterly destroy the room. That will be the first time she uploads footage of herself performing to the internet. Her life will never be the same.

O.K., maybe things won't change for her overnight, but you get my point. Suddenly her material will be available to the world. Whenever anyone wants to see her set, boom! It's right there on the internet. Anyone — her friends, bookers, fellow comedians or maybe just millions of strangers — can search for it or stumble upon it. They can hit "play" and the set will immediately begin and run as seamlessly as it did that night at the comedy club. If this happens frequently enough (and it does), then her life and career will change. Then she gets the ultimate break: being invited to do the same set on "The Ellen DeGeneres Show." Instant fame.

This kind of thing has happened, countless times. And not just to comics but also to magicians, singers and people who were embarrassed on camera but managed to monetize their shame. It will happen again. But it may not happen much longer if the chairman of the Federal Communications Commission, Ajit Pai, follows through on his plan to roll back the network neutrality rules that ensure that anyone who puts something on the internet has a fair shot at finding a life-changing audience.

The current rules, which have been in place since 2015, ensure that internet service providers treat all data — websites, shows, emails — the same. That means nobody has to pay extra money to make sure his or her content loads quickly. This fair internet, where everyone from an amateur comedian to a celebrity to a huge media company plays by the same rules, means you don't need a lot of money or the backing of someone with power to share your content with the world.

To understand how consequential this is, imagine a young woman walking into the HBO offices and saying, "Hi, I'm an awkward black girl and I think I have some pretty hilarious misadventures that you should make into a TV show!" HBO's only question probably would have been, "How did you get in here?" Now picture this: "Hi, I'm Issa Rae. I have hundreds of thousands of YouTube subscribers and hundreds of millions of YouTube views. And I'm an awkward black girl." HBO's question: "When can you start?" I'm exaggerating. But only slightly. Issa Rae started the web series "The Misadventures of Awkward Black Girl" on YouTube in 2011. Thanks in large part to its success, six years later, her comedy series, "Insecure," is set to air for a third season on HBO. It's hard to imagine this happening in a world without net neutrality.

Net neutrality is crucial to the careers of comedians like Ms. Rae and me, but it also allows content about more serious subjects to find an audience, without the endorsement or approval of traditional media gatekeepers.

When the activists Alicia Garza, Opal Tometi and Patrisse Cullors started using the hashtag #BlackLivesMatter to discuss the killing of the unarmed black teenager Trayvon Martin, it began trending worldwide, eventually anchoring the modern movement against police brutality against African-Americans. It's a reminder that the people providing the sharpest and most current analysis are often not employed by major media. This is still the case: Puerto Rico recovery updates? I'm going with @RosaClemente. Insightful takes on diversity in Hollywood? @ReignOfApril has them all. Weirdly perfect gifs and memes to make it through the daily news about the Trump administration? @ParkerMolloy has got me every time.

Thanks to our current net neutrality rules, when people like this take their genius beyond Twitter, to the rest of the internet, they don't have to worry about whether it's in a pay-to-play internet "fast lane" that makes access to certain types of content easier. They're in the same lane as everyone else, because net neutrality means there can be only one lane. ISPs can't do anything to stand between them and the people they want to speak to, and we all benefit.

The exchange of information and ideas that takes place on the internet is more important now than ever. To protect it, we need to keep the current net neutrality rules in places. We need them to ensure that people working to make the world better can reach their intended audiences. We need them to ensure that artists everywhere continue to have a platform through which we can discover their work. Right now, the internet is a level playing field. The question the Trump administration needs to answer is: Why would you want to change that?

W. KAMAU BELL IS THE HOST OF THE CNN DOCU-SERIES "UNITED SHADES OF AMERICA" AND THE AUTHOR OF "THE AWKWARD THOUGHTS OF W. KAMAU BELL."

F.C.C. Plan to Roll Back Net Neutrality Worries Small Businesses

BY TIFFANY HSU | NOV. 22, 2017

DAVID CALLICOTT needs to be online to run his small company, Good-Light Natural Candles in San Francisco.

Dozens of orders from wholesale customers like Whole Foods and Bed Bath & Beyond are relayed online each day to fulfillment warehouses, which send out Mr. Callicott's paraffin-free candles. The Good-Light website accounts for 15 percent of its sales, which could reach $1.5 million this year; the e-commerce behemoth Amazon makes up another 10 percent. And many of the company's business documents are stored in cloud-based data centers.

PETER PRATO FOR THE NEW YORK TIMES

David Callicott runs a small company, GoodLight Natural Candles, in San Francisco. "For such an analog product, we're heavily reliant on the digital world and the internet for our day-to-day operations," he said. "The internet, the speed of it, our entire business revolves around that."

But the costs of doing business on the internet may be about to rise.

A proposal on Tuesday by the Federal Communications Commission would undo so-called net neutrality rules that barred high-speed internet service providers from adjusting website delivery speeds and charging customers extra for access.

Without those regulations, GoodLight and other smaller businesses fear they may not have a level digital playing field to compete against deep-pocketed industry giants that could pay to get an edge online.

"For such an analog product, we're heavily reliant on the digital world and the internet for our day-to-day operations," said Mr. Callicott, who helped found the company nearly eight years ago and now works with three other full-time employees. "The internet, the speed of it, our entire business revolves around that."

The regulations, established by the F.C.C. in 2015, have heavyweights on both sides of the debate. Internet giants like Google and Amazon say that net neutrality preserves free speech; telecom titans like AT&T and Verizon warn that the existing rules put a chokehold on free-market commerce. In a blog post on Tuesday, Comcast's chief executive, David N. Watson, wrote that his company "does not and will not block, throttle, or discriminate against lawful content."

Internet service providers say that the proposal would lead to a better variety of services for online customers and more innovation in the industry.

For small businesses, a rollback could fundamentally change how, and whether, they do business. Many started online or turned to e-commerce to expand their thin margins.

"Things are already difficult enough as it is for a small businesses," Mr. Callicott said. "You're busy enough just keeping your company running, trying to grow and succeed or just stay alive, that you don't have the resources or the time to contemplate how to prepare for something like this."

In the United States, 99.7 percent of all businesses have fewer than 500 employees, according to government statistics. Of those, nearly 80 percent, or more than 23 million enterprises, are one-person operations.

More than a quarter of small firms said they planned to expand their e-commerce platforms in 2017, according to the National Small Business Association.

In August, the American Sustainable Business Council and other small business groups published an open letter to the F.C.C. on behalf of more than 500 small businesses in the country. Weakening or undoing net neutrality protections would be "disastrous" for American businesses, according to the letter.

"The open internet has made it possible for us to rely on a free market where each of us has the chance to bring our best business ideas to the world without interference or seeking permission from any gatekeeper first," the groups wrote.

Many entrepreneurs worried that, without net neutrality provisions, internet providers would wield their increased power to control how businesses reach consumers.

Online consumers are a demanding crowd. Research from a Google subsidiary suggested that visitors who have to wait more than 3 seconds for a mobile site to load will abandon their search 53 percent of the time.

Critics of the F.C.C. proposal say internet service providers could manipulate traffic speeds to establish a "fast lane" of sorts or cap or block access to certain sites, charging fees to lift the restrictions. Small enterprises would struggle to pay, leaving them at a commercial disadvantage, they said.

Independent contractors like Clayton Cowles, who works in upstate New York, could also be vulnerable.

Mr. Cowles draws the text for comic book publishers including Marvel, DC and Image, and has worked on Batman, Star Wars and other popular series.

Each month, he pays Spectrum, his internet service provider, $90.70 for the company's most powerful service package, which is supposed to allow him to send enormous digital documents within seconds. Instead, his files sometimes take 15 minutes to be delivered, he said.

A more deeply deregulated Spectrum is one of his "greatest fears," he said.

"They pretty much have a monopoly," he said. "I'm stuck with them."

Changes in net neutrality regulations could also affect the freelancers, franchisees and temporary workers who earn a living doing piecemeal work in the so-called gig economy. Nearly a quarter of American adults made money last year using digital platforms to take on a job or a task, selling something online or renting out their properties using a home-sharing site like Airbnb, according to the Pew Research Center.

A pay-for-play internet system could also be problematic for Codecademy, an education company founded in 2011. Its services include courses on tech-related subjects like data analysis, website design and coding language — all conducted online.

But Zach Sims, the company's chief executive, said that students, many of whom are aspiring entrepreneurs, would suffer most.

"They'll perceive it as an unfair playing field," he said. "As every industry is upended by tech, the barrier to entry is knowing what technology is and how to implement it, but this adds another level of confusion, making the hurdle even higher for normal businesses to participate."

NIRAJ CHOKSHI CONTRIBUTED REPORTING.

Net Neutrality Hits a Nerve, Eliciting Intense Reactions

BY CECILIA KANG | NOV. 28, 2017

WASHINGTON — It usually doesn't take much to get people on the internet worked up. To get them really worked up, make the topic internet regulation.

In the week since the Federal Communications Commission released a plan to scrap existing rules for internet delivery, more than 200,000 phone calls, organized through online campaigns, have been placed to Congress in protest. An additional 500,000 comments have been left on the agency's website. On social media sites like Twitter and Reddit, the issue has been a leading topic of discussion.

In some cases, views on the sweeping change, which would repeal landmark regulations meant to ensure an open internet, have turned into personal attacks. The agency's chairman, Ajit Pai, said threatening calls and emails had poured into his home and his wife's work. An image of a protest poster with his children's names was posted online and spread widely. Ethnic slurs aimed at Mr. Pai, whose parents immigrated from India, littered his Twitter feed.

There are also echoes of the 2016 presidential election, with accusations that not all of the reaction is coming from Americans. The federal agency is for the first time dealing with a powerful technology foe as automated software, known as bots, appears to have sent many comments to the site, according to data researchers.

And at least 400,000 comments about the issue since April on the F.C.C. site appear to have originated from an apartment in St. Petersburg, Russia, the agency said. It is unclear whether the emails did originate from there, or were made to look as if they did.

But none of that has overshadowed the heated reaction to the agency's proposal.

"There doesn't seem to be middle ground on this issue," said John Beahn, a lawyer at Skadden Arps who specializes in regulation.

At the center of the debate is whether telecom companies like AT&T and Verizon should be able to charge internet sites for delivering their data to consumers' homes. In 2015, the F.C.C. voted to prohibit those charges, in a policy often called net neutrality.

But Mr. Pai, a Republican nominated for the chairmanship by President Trump, said the regulations were heavy-handed and prevented telecom companies from pursuing new business models. His proposal, by stripping away the existing rules, would allow telecom companies to charge websites to deliver their data at higher speeds.

In a speech on Tuesday, Mr. Pai addressed some of the concerns that have been voiced since he released his proposal, pointing specifically to comments by celebrities like Cher and Kumail Nanjiani of "Silicon Valley." He said their tweets warning that his rules would lead to authoritarianism and a handout to big cable companies were "utterly absurd."

"I'd like to cut through hysteria and hot air and speak in plain terms about the plan," Mr. Pai said, adding that the plan would bring back the regulation-free policy that helped the internet thrive. He said big tech companies might be a bigger threat to online speech than telecom companies.

The proposal is expected to be approved at a meeting of the five F.C.C. commissioners on Dec. 14. The two other Republican commissioners have already expressed their support for Mr. Pai.

The 2015 rules also elicited strong interest. The F.C.C. site was overwhelmed with comments after a monologue from the late-night host John Oliver went viral online. Some people who wanted the stronger rules blocked the driveway of the chairman at the time, Tom Wheeler, to try to persuade him to change the agency's plan.

Big web companies like Google and Netflix played activist roles as well, supporting the stronger rules. They argued that telecom companies should not be able to split sites into fast lanes and slow lanes, because that would allow them to become a sort of gatekeeper for information and entertainment. In addition, they say, it would hurt start-ups without the money to pay for the faster lanes.

Mr. Pai, who opposed the rules as a commissioner in 2015, gave broad outlines of his plans early this year. For months, comments to the F.C.C. website piled up, to more than 20 million. President Barack Obama's clean power plan, perhaps his biggest policy change at the Environmental Protection Agency, attracted 4.3 million comments over six months.

But the intensity has increased even more since Mr. Pai released the details of the proposal — perhaps in part because few people expected him to try to strip all of the existing rules.

"We never expected this," wrote Craig Moffett, an analyst at the research firm MoffettNathanson.

Lawmakers, celebrities, founders of start-ups and consumers have continued to hash out the debate into this week.

Conservative groups like FreedomWorks and the Competitive Enterprise Institute praised the rollback. The radio host Rush Limbaugh defended Mr. Pai's plan on Monday in an online post. He dismissed concerns by supporters of the rules, whom he described as liberal "millennials and tech bloggers."

"What the tech bloggers and the left don't like is that there are options and that there is a freedom in the marketplace and that people can choose superior service if they're willing to pay for it," Mr. Limbaugh said. "And if somebody's willing to pay for superior service, the providers had better provide it."

Public interest groups like Free Press and organizations like Mozilla, the nonprofit behind the popular Firefox browser, said they were prepared to file suit against the plan as soon as the vote on Dec. 14.

"The action hit a nerve because the internet is central to the vast majority of people's daily lives, and so people were very eager to understand what was happening over the weekend," said Denelle Dixon, chief legal officer for Mozilla.

The reaction from the biggest tech companies, however, has been noticeably subdued. Instead of forceful pleas from their executives, like those in years past on this issue, they are largely speaking through their trade group, the Internet Association, which has expressed disappointment over Mr. Pai's plan.

"Internet companies are firm supporters of the 2015 Open Internet Order and will continue our push for strong, enforceable net neutrality rules going forward," said Noah Theran, a spokesman for the Internet Association. "We are reviewing the draft order and weighing our legal options."

Taking their place are start-ups such as Airbnb, Twitter and Reddit, which joined dozens of smaller start-ups on Monday warning Mr. Pai that the rules would hurt innovation and the economy.

Sorting out the real individual commenters from fake or automated accounts is far more tricky. The F.C.C. said it did not have the resources to investigate every comment on its site.

Eric Schneiderman, the New York attorney general, said that after a six-month investigation, his office had found that the identities of tens of thousands of state residents were fraudulently used to post comments to the F.C.C.

"If law enforcement can't investigate and (where appropriate) prosecute when it happens on this scale," Mr. Schneiderman said, "the door is open for it to happen again and again."

How Repealing Net Neutrality Will Hurt Consumers

LETTERS TO THE EDITOR | NOV. 29, 2017

To the Editor:

In "Net Neutrality Facing Full Repeal in F.C.C. Plan" (news article, Nov. 21), we learn that in a speech in April the Federal Communications Commission chairman, Ajit Pai, speaking of the creation of net neutrality, claimed that "we decided to abandon successful policies solely because of hypothetical harms." Net neutrality gives a level playing field for content providers and allows consumers to select any content from the web.

Contrary to Mr. Pai's claim, the harms are not hypothetical. In early 2014, before the current net neutrality rules were adopted, Comcast slowed data from Netflix to a crawl. Netflix paid Comcast and the problem was resolved.

But suppose Netflix were unwilling or unable to pay Comcast. Theoretically the consumer who wanted Netflix could select a different internet service provider, but in reality there is often no or very little choice of I.S.P.s. Under the current rules, Comcast could not slow data based on the content provider.

Without net neutrality, I.S.P.s become gatekeepers of which content gets to their customers. This could leave many small businesses without the ability to reach their customers and many customers without choices. Furthermore, I.S.P. owners could decide to block content from a political party that did not align with their political views.

Gatekeepers have a great deal of power, and without regulation can abuse that power. Mr. Pai's refusal to acknowledge this is very dangerous for both the economy and our democracy.

ETHAN ANNIS, SAN FRANCISCO

To the Editor:

Re "F.C.C. Releases Plan to Repeal Net Neutrality" (front page, Nov. 22): On the expected demise of net neutrality, as with the removal of so many rights and privileges, the authorities responsible for these losses present them as giving more people more choices: Ajit Pai is removing net neutrality "so that consumers can buy the service plan that's best for them." Similarly, repealing the Affordable Care Act will provide consumers with more choices; expanding charter schools will give parents more choices about where to educate their children.

Take away a right, and call it a choice: That'll confuse them!

KATHY HIEATT, BROOKLYN

To the Editor:

The telecoms and cable companies have for years tried to create a "walled garden" around content, controlling users' access. Now faced with the further disaggregation of content, they are seeking government intervention to abet their monopolies by dissolving net neutrality.

If this move is truly about innovation and investment, then the Federal Communications Commission should work with Congress to encourage and allow community broadband initiatives. The internet should not be turned into a "printing press," with the control over information resting in the hands of a few corporations that are more interested in profits than the free and creative flow of ideas.

TOM HICKS, RESTON, VA.

THE WRITER WAS THE FOUNDER OF DISCOVERY CHANNEL ONLINE.

Why Concerns About Net Neutrality Are Overblown

OPINION | BY KEN ENGELHART | DEC. 4, 2017

TORONTO — The Federal Communications Commission is planning to jettison its network neutrality rules, and many Americans are distraught. Such a move, the Electronic Frontier Foundation warned, "invites a future where only the largest internet, cable and telephone companies survive, while every start-up, small business and new innovator is crowded out — and the voices of nonprofits and ordinary individuals are suppressed."

Critics worry that getting rid of neutrality regulation will lead to a "two-tier" internet: Internet service providers will start charging fees to websites and apps, and slow down or block the sites that don't pay up. As a result, users will have unfettered access to only part of the internet, with the rest either inaccessible or slow.

Those fears are vastly overblown.

It's true that in the past, some service providers have threatened to charge websites. In 2005, during a previous phase in the net neutrality debate, the chief executive of SBC Communications said, "Now what they would like to do is use my pipes for free, but I ain't going to let them do that because we have spent this capital and we have to have a return on it."

Service providers have also blocked sites that competed with their own services. In 2004, the Madison River Telephone Company in North Carolina blocked Vonage to protect its own phone service from competition; it was fined by the F.C.C. for violating network neutrality rules. In 2012, AT&T let only some of its customers use the phone app FaceTime; after there were complaints to the F.C.C., it allowed all customers to use it.

These incidents are troubling for anyone who wants on open, neutral internet. But keep two things in mind. First, these are rare examples,

PETE RYAN

for a reason: The public blowback was fierce, scaring other providers from following suit. Second, blocking competitors to protect your own services is anticompetitive conduct that might well be stopped by antitrust laws without any need for network neutrality regulations.

Net-neutrality defenders also worry that some service providers could slow down high-data peer-to-peer traffic, like BitTorrent. And again, it has happened, most notably in 2007, when Comcast throttled some peer-to-peer file sharing. The F.C.C. declared this to be a violation of its network neutrality policy; Comcast got that policy overturned in court, though it also settled a class-action lawsuit by customers (the current net neutrality rule was put in place by the Obama administration).

But even today, service providers can and do throttle peer-to-peer sites, as a necessary network management technique — something explicitly allowed by the rules. Some university networks also slow peer-to-peer traffic, so that other kinds of traffic are not slowed down. This has nothing to do with service providers slowing down websites that have not paid a fee.

So why am I not worried? I worked for a telecommunications company for 25 years, and whatever one may think about corporate control over the internet, I know that it simply is not in service providers' interests to throttle access to what consumers want to see. Neutral broadband access is a cash cow; why would they kill it?

Even if they wanted to, service providers would have a hard time extorting money from huge companies like Google and Netflix, because each service provider needs Google and its billions of users a lot more than Google needs it. Service providers could try to go after smaller websites, but they don't have much money to pay.

And there's still competition: Some markets may have just one cable provider, but phone companies offer increasingly comparable internet access — so if the cable provider slowed down or blocked some sites, the phone company could soak up the affected customers simply by promising not to do so.

Recently, net neutrality proponents have pointed to Portugal as an example of their nightmare scenario. A mobile carrier there offers various internet packages — one optimized for users who like video, others who like email and so on. What the carrier does not do is offer only those things, precisely because no consumer is likely to buy just video or just email (and in any case, Portugal is governed by the European Union's net-neutrality rules).

The internet did not start out as a neutral invention. Instead, neutrality was an organic outcome of a competitive market. In the early days of the commercial internet, AOL and @Home had "walled gardens" of content that users could get to more easily, but over time service providers stopped favoring sites and just gave customers fast, neutral internet connections. No government policy created that outcome.

The good news is that we will soon have a real-world experiment to show who is right and who is wrong. The United States will get rid of its rules, and the European Union and Canada will keep their stringent regulations. In two years, will the American internet be slower, less innovative and split into two tiers, leaving Canadians to enjoy their fast and neutral net?

Or, as I suspect, will the two markets remain very similar — proving that this whole agonized debate has been a giant waste of time? Let's check back in 2019.

KEN ENGELHART, A LAWYER SPECIALIZING IN COMMUNICATIONS LAW, IS A SENIOR ADVISER FOR STRATEGYCORP, AN ADJUNCT PROFESSOR AT OSGOODE HALL LAW SCHOOL AND A SENIOR FELLOW AT THE C. D. HOWE INSTITUTE.

Net Neutrality Protests Move Online, Yet Big Tech Is Quiet

BY CECILIA KANG, DAISUKE WAKABAYASHI, NICK WINGFIELD AND MIKE ISAAC | DEC. 12, 2017

PROTESTS TO PRESERVE net neutrality, or rules that ensure equal access to the internet, migrated online on Tuesday, with numerous online companies posting calls on their sites for action to stop a vote later this week.

Reddit, Etsy and Kickstarter were among the sites warning that the proposal at the Federal Communications Commission to roll back so-called net neutrality rules would fundamentally change the way the internet is experienced. Kickstarter, the crowdfunding site, cleared its entire home screen for a sparse white screen reading "Defend Net Neutrality" in large letters. Reddit, the popular online message board, pushed in multiple ways on its site for keeping the rules, including a pop-up box on its home screen.

But the online protests also highlighted how the biggest tech companies, such as Facebook and Google, have taken a back seat in the debate about protecting net neutrality, rules that prohibit internet service providers like AT&T and Comcast from blocking or slowing sites or for charging people or companies for faster speeds of particular sites. For the most part, the large tech companies did not engage in the protest on Tuesday. In the past, the companies have played a leading role in supporting the rules.

Harold Feld, a senior vice president at Public Knowledge, a nonprofit group that supports net neutrality, said the biggest tech companies were less vocal because they were facing more regulatory battles than in past years. Social media sites have been criticized for allowing foreign actors to interfere in the presidential election of 2016. The biggest tech companies also face complaints from some lawmakers that they have become too large and powerful.

"First, the major tech companies are very aware that Washington has turned hostile," Mr. Feld said. "In this environment, the big tech companies try to keep a low profile and play defense rather than take positions that draw attention.

"So with the dangers of standing up in D.C. greater, their existential concerns about net neutrality reduced because of their own massive size and a desire not to spook investors, it is unsurprising that Silicon Valley giants have melted into the background and have preferred to work through their trade associations," he said.

There also does not appear to be much chance of their winning the debate right now. The three Republican members of the F.C.C., who make up a majority of commissioners at the agency, have committed to roll back the landmark broadband rules created during the Obama administration.

But consumers and the start-ups that participated in protests on Tuesday say they are gearing up for a long fight. They expect lawsuits to challenge the change, and plan to push Congress to pass a law ensuring an open internet.

Here is how several of the biggest companies have handled the issue in recent months.

GOOGLE BACKS OFF

Google has kept a pretty low profile in the recent net neutrality debate. The company issued a statement last month when the proposed changes were announced, saying that the current rules were "working well" and that it was "disappointed" by the new proposal. But for the most part, the company has been working within the Internet Association, an industry group that includes Facebook, Amazon and other large online companies.

It's a restrained approach compared with Google's aggressive lobbying campaign in 2006 when Sergey Brin, one of the company's co-founders, went to Capitol Hill to argue for the importance of net neutrality. In 2010, Google teamed up with Verizon to lay out a vision for how net neutrality could work, advocating against allowing internet service providers to provide fast lanes to people who pay more. However, the proposal was criticized by advocates of an open internet because it excluded wireless connectivity and new services from broadband providers.

APPLE ENTERS THE DEBATE

Apple is a newcomer to the net neutrality debate. It made its first filing to the F.C.C. on the issue in August. It espoused a position largely in line with other internet giants, arguing against the creation of fast lanes and emphasizing the importance of an open internet.

Apple's public opposition to the proposed changes also reflects the growing network of services on offer from the company including Apple Music, a streaming music service that also offers video content, and potentially an internet video service to rival Netflix.

Timothy D. Cook, Apple's chief executive, said in a statement that all internet service providers should treat all data on the internet equally.

"Equal treatment is critical to innovation in a digital economy and to democracy," he said. "If the F.C.C. doesn't provide this basic protection, we urge Congress to intervene."

FACEBOOK FOCUSES ELSEWHERE

During the last day of online protest in support of the rules this past summer, Mark Zuckerberg and Sheryl Sandberg, Facebook's leaders, posted defiant statements to their personal Facebook pages.

But the executives have been pretty quiet on the issue in recent months. The company's focus in Washington has been more concentrated on fallout from its handling of Russian-linked propaganda used during the 2016 presidential election.

This week, Facebook offered a statement from Erin Egan, a policy spokeswoman, about the F.C.C. plans:

"Facebook has always supported the kind of strong net neutrality protections that will ensure the internet remains open for everyone,"

Ms. Egan said. "We are disappointed by the F.C.C.'s decision to remove these protections, and we stand ready to work with policymakers on a framework that will protect a free and open internet."

MICROSOFT KEEPS LOW PROFILE

Microsoft sent a 23-page letter to the commission later in July outlining the company's argument that the commission should not change its stance on net neutrality. "Now is not the time for the commission to abandon 15 years of progress toward protecting the economic future of our country," the letter said. "Now is not the time for the commission to abandon its open internet rules."

The company has otherwise kept a relatively low profile on the issue. On Nov. 28, Brad Smith, Microsoft's president and chief legal officer, tweeted that "Microsoft believes in preserving the open internet & opposes weakening net neutrality protections."

AMAZON TAKES CASE TO F.C.C.

Amazon representatives have been lobbying F.C.C. commissioners and staff in person, with visits on Nov. 29 and last Wednesday. The latter included a meeting between Ajit Pai, the F.C.C. chairman, and Darren Achord, an Amazon senior public policy manager.

"During the meetings, we stated that Amazon has long supported net neutrality protections to ensure our customers can enjoy an open internet, and we emphasized that the company remains committed to that position," Gerard Waldron, a lawyer who represents Amazon and participated in the meeting, wrote in an account filed with the F.C.C.

"We stressed the need for enforceable, bright-line rules to protect the open internet and guard against anti-consumer and anti-competitive activities," he wrote, adding that Amazon opposed the commission's proposed change.

NETFLIX TURNS DOWN THE VOLUME

Netflix, once among the most vocal of net neutrality boosters, is perhaps the most conspicuous in its relative silence. In recent months, the company's chief executive, Reed Hastings, has said net neutrality is no longer the company's "primary battle," partly because Netflix is now large enough that it can secure the deals it needs with internet access providers to ensure its service is delivered smoothly to customers.

On Nov. 21, the company posted a note on its primary Twitter account in support of net neutrality.

One Twitter user responded by saying the company should do more "to tell people how it will potentially affect them."

Jonathan Friedland, a spokesman for Netflix, said this week that the company did not have anything to add to its earlier statements opposing the F.C.C.'s actions.

F.C.C. Repeals Net Neutrality Rules

BY CECILIA KANG | DEC. 14, 2017

WASHINGTON — The Federal Communications Commission voted on Thursday to dismantle rules regulating the businesses that connect consumers to the internet, granting broadband companies the power to potentially reshape Americans' online experiences.

The agency scrapped the so-called net neutrality regulations that prohibited broadband providers from blocking websites or charging for higher-quality service or certain content. The federal government will also no longer regulate high-speed internet delivery as if it were a utility, like phone service.

The action reversed the agency's 2015 decision, during the Obama administration, to have stronger oversight over broadband providers as Americans have migrated to the internet for most communications. It reflected the view of the Trump administration and the new F.C.C. chairman that unregulated business will eventually yield innovation and help the economy.

It will take weeks for the repeal to go into effect, so consumers will not see any of the potential changes right away. But the political and legal fight started immediately. Numerous Democrats on Capitol Hill called for a bill that would reestablish the rules, and several Democratic state attorneys general, including Eric T. Schneiderman of New York, said they would file a suit to stop the change.

Several public interest groups including Public Knowledge and the National Hispanic Media Coalition also promised to file a suit. The Internet Association, the trade group that represents big tech firms such as Google and Facebook, said it also was considering legal action.

The commission's chairman, Ajit Pai, vigorously defended the repeal before the vote. He said the rollback of the rules would eventually benefit consumers because broadband providers like AT&T and Comcast could offer them a wider variety of service options. His two fellow Republican commissioners also supported the change, giving them a 3-to-2 majority.

"We are helping consumers and promoting competition," Mr. Pai said. "Broadband providers will have more incentive to build networks, especially to underserved areas."

The discarding of the net neutrality regulations is the most significant and controversial action by the F.C.C. under Mr. Pai. In his first 11 months as chairman, he has lifted media ownership limits, eased caps on how much broadband providers can charge business customers and cut back on a low-income broadband program that was slated to be expanded to nationwide carriers.

His plan for the net neutrality rules, first outlined early this year, set off a flurry of opposition. The issue has bubbled up occasionally for more than a decade, with the debate getting more intense over the years as digital services have become more ingrained in everyday life.

Critics of the changes say that consumers will have more difficulty accessing content online and that start-ups will have to pay to reach consumers. In the past week, there have been hundreds of protests across the country, and many websites have encouraged users to speak up against the repeal.

In front of a room packed with reporters and television cameras from the major networks, the two Democratic commissioners warned of consumer harms to come from the changes.

Mignon Clyburn, one of the Democratic commissioners, presented two accordion folders full of letters protesting the changes, and accused the three Republican commissioners of defying the wishes of millions of Americans by ceding their oversight authority.

"I dissent, because I am among the millions outraged," said Ms. Clyburn. "Outraged, because the F.C.C. pulls its own teeth, abdicating responsibility to protect the nation's broadband consumers."

Brendan Carr, a Republican commissioner, said it was a "great day" and dismissed critics' "apocalyptic" warnings.

"I'm proud to end this two-year experiment with heavy-handed regulation," Mr. Carr said.

During Mr. Pai's speech before the vote, security guards entered the meeting room at the F.C.C. headquarters and told everyone to evacuate. The commissioners were ushered out a back door. The agency did not say what had caused the evacuation, other than Mr. Pai saying it had been done "on advice of security." The hearing restarted a short time later.

Despite all the uproar, it is unclear how much will eventually change for internet users. Major telecom companies like AT&T and Comcast, as well as two of the industry's major trade groups, have promised consumers that their experiences online would not change.

Mr. Pai and his Republican colleagues have echoed the comments of the telecom companies, which have told regulators that because of the limits to their business imposed by the rules, they weren't expanding and upgrading their networks as quickly as they wanted.

"There is a lot of misinformation that this is the 'end of the world as we know it' for the internet," Comcast's senior executive vice president, David Cohen, wrote in a blog post this week. "Our internet service is not going to change."

But with the F.C.C. making clear that it will no longer oversee the behavior of broadband providers, telecom experts said, the companies could feel freer to come up with new offerings, such as faster tiers of service for online businesses willing and able to pay for it. Some of those costs could be passed on to consumers.

Those experts also said that such prioritization could stifle certain political voices or give the telecom conglomerates with media assets an edge over their rivals.

Consumer groups, start-ups and many small businesses said there have already been examples of net neutrality violations by companies, such as when AT&T blocked FaceTime on iPhones using its network.

These critics of Mr. Pai, who was nominated by President Trump, said there isn't enough competition in the broadband market to trust that the companies will try to offer the best services. The rule changes, they believe, give providers incentive to begin charging websites to reach consumers.

"Let's remember why we have these rules in the first place," said Michael Beckerman, president of the Internet Association, the trade group. "There is little competition in the broadband service market."

Dozens of Democratic lawmakers, and some Republicans, have pushed for Congress to pass a law on the issue.

One Republican commissioner, Mike O'Reilly, said he supported a law created by Congress for net neutrality. But he said any law should be less restrictive than the 2015 rules, protecting the ability of companies to charge for faster lanes, a practice known as "paid prioritization."

Any legislative action appears to be far off, however, and numerous online companies warned that the changes approved on Thursday should be taken seriously.

"If we don't have net neutrality protections that enforce tenets of fairness online, you give internet service providers the ability to choose winners and losers," Steve Huffman, chief executive of Reddit, said in an interview. "This is not hyperbole."

In Protests of Net Neutrality Repeal, Teenage Voices Stood Out

BY CECILIA KANG | DEC. 20, 2017

WASHINGTON — When Anooha Dasari, 16, heard the federal government was about to kill rules that guaranteed an open internet, she contacted her United States representatives for the first time, asking them to stop the action.

The Mundelein, Ill., high school junior then passed around a link to classmates for a website that automatically placed calls, web comments and emails to the Federal Communications Commission, the agency that was moving to repeal the so-called net neutrality rules. When the F.C.C. voted last week on the rollback, Ms. Dasari stayed glued to her smartphone for updates while taking her American government class.

"For research, for news, to communicate with friends, the internet

LYNDON FRENCH FOR THE NEW YORK TIMES

"The internet is a big part of my life," said Anooha Dasari, 16, a high school junior, adding that the repeal of net neutrality is "dangerous."

is a big part of my life," Ms. Dasari said. "It has formulated my personality, opinions and political ideology. If it is controlled, my generation of students could be inclined to be just on one part of the spectrum. That's dangerous."

Millions of Americans have been caught up in a bitter debate over the repeal of net neutrality rules that prevented broadband providers from blocking websites or demanding fees to reach consumers. But the most vocal and committed activity may have come from generation internet, the digitally savvy teenagers in middle and high school who grew up with an open internet.

The repeal of net neutrality has gotten many of these teens politically engaged for the first time, with fears that the dismantling of rules could open the door for broadband providers like AT&T and Comcast to distort the experience of accessing anything online with equal ease. For them, a dry issue that has often been hard to understand outside of policy circles in Washington has become a cause to rally around.

"For students that have used an internet that is open and without tolls their whole life, as complicated as net neutrality is, kids can get their heads around it pretty easily," said John Lewis, the head of Gunston School, a private high school in Centreville, Md.

Net neutrality's repeal will not take effect for several weeks. Internet service providers including AT&T and Comcast have promised they won't block or throttle sites or create fast lanes for certain content. And several efforts are underway to scale back the rollback, including the introduction of a congressional bill and potential lawsuits.

The opposition by many teenagers is rooted in how they are among the most avid users of the internet and smartphones. Virtually all youth between ages 13 and 17 own or have access to a smartphone and 94 percent use social media, according to an April 2017 study by The Associated Press-NORC Center for Public Affairs Research. Many are gaining access to devices at younger ages, with 98 percent of children from newborn to 8 years old accessing a mobile device at home, compared with 52 percent in 2011.

SAM HODGSON FOR THE NEW YORK TIMES

Protesters in front of a Verizon store in New York this month demonstrated against the Federal Communications Commission's repeal of net neutrality rules.

Many became digital users when net neutrality was in effect. Net neutrality has existed in various forms since about 2006, when the F.C.C. first created open internet guidelines for broadband providers known as the "Four Internet Freedoms." In 2015, the F.C.C. declared that broadband had become utility-like and deserved extra government oversight. Since 2006, more and more children began using Netflix, Snapchat, Instagram, YouTube and all manner of other apps and online services.

In the days before the F.C.C. voted on net neutrality repeal last week, children and teenagers organized protests in Sioux Falls, S.D., and Keene, N.H. They wrote letters and sent tweets to F.C.C. commissioners and volunteered for texting and phone campaigns to push members of Congress to use their authority to overturn or dilute the F.C.C. decision.

Alli Webb, 18, a senior at Gunston, missed school last week ahead of the F.C.C. vote with permission from Mr. Lewis and her parents. With three other students, she drove two hours to downtown Washington to stand in front of a Verizon store during lunch hour. There, she hollered slogans to save net neutrality rules with signs that read "Stop F.C.C.!" and "Equal Opportunity: Still Loading."

"This is really bad for technology, innovation and our future," said Ms. Webb, who wants to study computer science in college. "This is going to totally change the internet." She said she feared start-ups would have to submit to the demands of internet service providers to showcase their sites, which could hold back entrepreneurs.

At Southside High School in Rockville Centre, N.Y., net neutrality dominated conversation in the lunchroom last week and throughout the day of the vote, last Thursday as students checked for updates.

"I've met lots of friends on Instagram and I communicate with my mom and with all my friends at least 10 times a day on social media," said Matthew Baxley, 15, a 10th grader who recently participated in a texting effort to protest the repeal. "The internet is at the center of a lot of what I do and care about."

Some teachers had to make adjustments. Laurie Crowe, a high school history teacher in Kyle, Tex., tried to give an exam to 11th graders at Lehman High School last Thursday but couldn't get her students off their phones and laptops. She was surprised to find them streaming the F.C.C. vote. Eventually, she postponed the exam so they could watch the five commissioners cast their votes and explain their positions.

When the F.C.C. chairman, Ajit Pai, cast the final vote to dismantle the rules, students slammed their laptops shut and tore off their earphones in disappointment, Ms. Crowe said.

"These kids felt very indignant and betrayed by this decision because they feel entitled to information and the internet," she said.

Ms. Dasari remains determined to fight. She said she would continue to push lawmakers to salvage open internet rules through legislation and she is following the news for lawsuits challenging the repeal.

"I will tweet and email and call and stay in the process," she said. "We have time and we won't go away."

States Push Back After Net Neutrality Repeal

BY CECILIA KANG | JAN. 11, 2018

WASHINGTON — A new front is opening in the battle to restore so-called net neutrality rules: state legislatures.

Lawmakers in at least six states, including California and New York, have introduced bills in recent weeks that would forbid internet providers to block or slow down sites or online services. Legislators in several other states, including North Carolina and Illinois, are weighing similar action.

They are responding to the Federal Communications Commission's vote last month to end regulations that barred internet service providers from creating slow and fast lanes for different sites and services. The new policy will go into effect in the coming weeks.

By passing their own law, the state lawmakers say, they would ensure that consumers would find the content of the choice, maintain a diversity of voices online and protect businesses from having to pay fees to reach users. And they might even have an effect beyond their states. California's strict auto emissions standards, for example, have been followed by a dozen other states, giving California major sway over the auto industry.

"There tends to be a follow-on effect, particularly when something happens in a big state like California," said Harold Feld, a senior vice president at nonprofit consumer group, Public Knowledge, which supports net neutrality efforts by the states.

Bills have also been introduced in Massachusetts, Nebraska, Rhode Island and Washington. The issue has also attracted some support in governor mansions. In Washington, for example, Gov. Jay Inslee reiterated his support for a state law in a speech this week.

"When Washington, D.C., takes away that protection, we must protect net neutrality for our people, for our businesses and for the virtues of free speech," Mr. Inslee, a Democrat, said.

But the bills are still in the early stages and could face roadblocks. Many similar efforts by states to restore broadband privacy rules that Congress repealed last year, have stalled or been scrapped.

And any such state law could be challenged in courts. The Federal Communications Commission's new order, which rolled back rules passed in 2015, blocks state and city governments from creating their own net neutrality laws. The commission said different state laws were too difficult for an internet service provider, like Verizon or Charter, to follow because the internet does not recognize state borders and transfers traffic between states.

"The internet is the ultimate form of interstate commerce, which is clearly only within the authority of the F.C.C.," said Bret Swanson, a fellow at the American Enterprise Institute who specializes in telecommunications policy.

But the state lawmakers argue that they have an obligation to protect consumers with net neutrality rules and that local governments can approve or deny requests by telecommunications providers to operate in their states. They also argue that it is unclear if the Federal Communications Commission can declare a blanket pre-emption of states, something they say Congress would have to do. In 2016, a federal court ruled against the commission's effort to pre-empt state laws related to municipal broadband networks.

"People should not be intimidated by the F.C.C. simply saying it has pre-emptive authority, and we need to dig into the sources of that claim, which are a lot weaker than the F.C.C. makes it out to be," said State Representative Drew Hansen, a Democrat who has introduced one of two net neutrality bills in Washington in recent weeks.

The Federal Communications Commission declined to comment but pointed to the section of its order that pre-empts states from creating their own net neutrality rules.

Supporters of net neutrality are attacking the agency's repeal of the 2015 rules in other ways as well. On Tuesday, Senator Chuck

Schumer of New York, the Democratic leader, announced that he had enough support to force a vote on a congressional resolution to bring back the rules. He gained an important Republican supporter, Senator Susan Collins of Maine, who said she would vote in favor of it. Such a measure is a long shot in the House, however, and would also need President Trump's signature.

"Net neutrality will be a major issue in the 2018 campaigns, and we are going to let everyone know where we stand and where they stand," Mr. Schumer said at a news conference, warning Republicans to vote in favor of the Democratic-led resolution.

In addition, lawsuits against the commission are expected shortly after the policy becomes official. Last week, a lobbying group for big technology companies including Facebook, Google and Netflix announced that it planned to join the lawsuits, giving the opposition substantial new resources. More than a dozen state attorneys general have also announced plans to sue the commission.

But state lawmakers say they cannot wait around to see what happens with those efforts.

State Representative Norma Smith, a Republican who introduced the other bill in Washington, said net neutrality was an important safeguard for small businesses that might not be able to pay internet service companies for fast speeds. Even though Republicans in Washington, D.C., supported the repeal, she said many Republicans in her state supported her bill.

"This is not a partisan issue here," Ms. Smith said. "Everyone is concerned about equal access to the internet and being able to participate in the 21st-century economy."

Kevin de León, a leader in the California Senate, said net neutrality would be a major issue in his campaign against Senator Dianne Feinstein in the Democratic primary this year. He said a net neutrality bill he had introduced, one of two in California, had the backing of tech companies and many consumers in his state. Ms. Feinstein has criticized the Federal Communications Commission's vote.

EVAN MCGLINN FOR THE NEW YORK TIMES

State Representative Norma Smith, a Republican, has introduced one of two net neutrality bills in Washington. "This is not a partisan issue here," she said.

"If the Trump administration won't protect consumers, the State of California will," Mr. de León said.

In New York, Assemblywoman Patricia Fahy, a Democrat, said a few internet service providers already had too much power over the marketplace and should not be given the ability to charge websites more for faster delivery to users.

This month, she introduced a bill that would hold back state telecom projects from broadband providers that blocked, throttled or gave priority to sites that paid for faster access. Legislators in Rhode Island and North Carolina have introduced or are considering similar bills that are more focused on government contracts than telecom law, they say.

"We are threading a needle here," Ms. Fahy said, "but this is the best way to get at consumer protection, because state projects are huge and this will really affect the internet service providers."

Flurry of Lawsuits Filed to Fight Repeal of Net Neutrality

BY CECILIA KANG | JAN. 16, 2018

WASHINGTON — The legal fight against the Federal Communications Commission's recent repeal of so-called net neutrality regulations began on Tuesday, with a flurry of lawsuits filed to block the agency's action.

One suit, filed by 21 state attorneys general, said the agency's actions broke federal law. The commission's rollback of net neutrality rules were "arbitrary and capricious," the attorneys general said, and a reversal of the agency's longstanding policy to prevent internet service providers from blocking or charging websites for faster delivery of content to consumers.

Mozilla, the nonprofit organization behind the Firefox web browser, said the new F.C.C. rules would harm internet entrepreneurs who could be forced to pay fees for faster delivery of their content and services to consumers. A similar argument was made by another group that filed a suit, the Open Technology Institute, a part of a liberal think tank, the New America Foundation.

Suits were also filed on Tuesday by Free Press and Public Knowledge, two public interest groups. Four of the suits were filed in the United States Court of Appeals for the District of Columbia Circuit. The Free Press suit was filed in the United States Court of Appeals for the First Circuit.

"The repeal of net neutrality would turn internet service providers into gatekeepers — allowing them to put profits over consumers while controlling what we see, what we do, and what we say online," said Eric T. Schneiderman, the attorney general of New York, who led the suit by the state officials.

The lawsuits have long been expected. The filings on Tuesday, petitions to begin the suits, kick off what is expected to be an extended legal and political debate about the future of internet policy.

Democrats have rallied to fight the F.C.C.'s repeal of net neutrality, which was passed in a 3-to-2 party line vote in December. The agency is

SASHA MASLOV FOR THE NEW YORK TIMES

Eric Schneiderman, New York State's attorney general, is leading a lawsuit to block the Federal Communications Commission's repeal of net neutrality regulations.

led by Ajit Pai, a Republican nominated by President Trump. All of the attorneys general involved in the suit filed on Tuesday are Democrats.

The lawsuits have the support of the Internet Association, a trade group representing big tech firms including Google and Netflix, giving the various legal challenges financial support and the clout of companies. The companies say internet service providers have the incentive to block and throttle their sites in order to garner extra fees.

The F.C.C. declined to comment on the suits. But it did point to a part of its order that prohibits legal challenges until the new rules are submitted into the federal registry. The F.C.C. is expected to enter the new rules into the federal registry in the coming days or weeks.

The states said they could file a petition to the United States Court of Appeals, starting the process to determine which court would hear the case. That is the action the attorneys general, as well as Mozilla and the Open Technology Institute, took on Tuesday.

The states that signed onto the lawsuit include California, Kentucky, Maryland, Massachusetts and Oregon, as well as the District of Columbia. Xavier Becerra, the California attorney general, said the decision to roll back the agency's declaration of broadband as a utility-like service will harm consumers.

"Internet access is a utility — just like water and electricity," Mr. Becerra said in a statement. "And every consumer has a right to access online content without interference or manipulation by their internet service provider."

In a release, Mr. Schneiderman said the agency's roll back disregarded a record of evidence that internet service providers' could harm consumers without rules. A similar argument was made by Mozilla.

"Ending net neutrality could end the internet as we know it," said Denelle Dixon, Mozilla's chief business and legal officer in a blog post. "That's why we are committed to fighting the order. In particular, we filed our petition today because we believe the recent F.C.C. decision violates both federal law as well as harms internet users and innovators."

The issue of net neutrality has been fought in court challenges twice before in the past decade. The rules adopted in 2015, which set rules that sites could not be blocked or throttled, were upheld by the United States Court of Appeals in 2016 after legal challenges by telecom companies. The F.C.C. vote in December was to roll back those 2015 rules.

The new lawsuits are among several efforts to restore net neutrality rules. On Tuesday, Senate Democrats announced they were one supporter away from winning a vote to restore net neutrality rules. All 49 members of their caucus, as well as one Republican, have signed on to a resolution to overturn the rules. A similar effort initiated in the House has the support of 80 members.

Success by members of Congress is unlikely, particularly in the House, where Speaker Paul D. Ryan, Republican of Wisconsin, would have to agree to bring the resolution to a vote. The president will also have to agree to the resolutions, if they were passed, but the White House has expressed its support of the rollback of net neutrality rules.

Washington Governor Signs First State Net Neutrality Bill

BY CECILIA KANG | MARCH 5, 2018

RESIDENTS OF WASHINGTON STATE are getting so-called net neutrality rules back, with the nation's first state law that prevents internet service providers from blocking and slowing down content online.

The law, signed on Monday by Gov. Jay Inslee, a Democrat, is the most sweeping state action so far against new federal rules that strip away regulations on how high-speed internet providers handle digital data. The dismantling of the nationwide rules, approved by the Federal Communications Commission last year, set off a fierce outcry from consumers and tech companies.

Opponents of the change in the federal regulations fear that without strong rules, internet service providers will create faster and slower lanes online to extract fees for better service. The F.C.C. said it got rid of the rules because they restrained broadband providers like Verizon and Comcast from experimenting with new business models and investing in new technologies.

The Washington State law, which goes into effect June 6, bars internet service providers from blocking websites or charging more for faster delivery of certain sites in a way that benefits the broadband company and partner websites.

The new law is one of several efforts to counter the F.C.C. change. Lawmakers in about two dozen states have introduced bills similar to Washington's. And multiple governors, including in New York and Montana, have signed executive actions that prohibit internet service providers with state contracts from blocking or slowing data on their lines.

But the law in Washington State goes further by immediately putting back into place consumer protections provided by the 2015 federal rules. The law passed with broad bipartisan support in the state legislature.

"At the core of our action today is consumer protection," Mr. Inslee said in an interview. "States need to act because under the Trump administration, we have seen citizens, including seven million in Washington, stripped of core protections like the open internet."

The actions by the states, both the executive actions and the new Washington law, are almost certain to end up in the courts. The F.C.C. has asserted it has the only authority to oversee broadband internet services, because the data on the internet passes across multiple state lines. In the rules it passed last year to reduce the regulations, the agency explicitly said states could not create their own rules.

Internet service providers could also sue Washington State to overturn its rules. The companies could also sue states whose governors have signed executive orders demanding net neutrality.

Glossary

Baby Bells Name for the Regional Bell Operating Companies, or the seven smaller companies (including AT&T, CenturyLink, and Verizon) into which the American Telephone and Telegraph (AT&T) Company was broken up following an antitrust suit brought on by the US Department of Justice.

balkanize To break up, divide, or compartmentalize.

bandwidth An electronic communications system's capacity for data transfer.

bipartisan Of, relating to, or involving members of both the Democratic and Republican parties.

broadband Of or relating to a high-speed electronic communications network.

court of appeals Title for the appellate courts in the United States federal court system, which review the decisions of district courts and whose decisions are subject to review by the Supreme Court.

dystopian Relating to an imaginary reality where individuals are dehumanized, denied rights, or live fearful lives.

egalitarian Asserting or promoting equality among people regardless of social or economic status.

Federal Communications Commission (F.C.C.) Independent agency of the United States government tasked with the regulation and oversight of all communications via radio, television, wire, satellite, and cable.

galvanize To excite or stimulate.

infrastructure The underlying framework of the public works or utility system of a country, state, or region.

insipid Lacking interesting or stimulating qualities.

internet A worldwide electronic communications network that connects many computer networks.

internet service provider (I.S.P.) An electronic communications company that provides customers with internet access.

merger The integration of two corporations or organizations into one, larger corporation or organization.

nefarious Blatantly evil or wicked.

paid prioritization The optimization of the speed of transfer of certain data in exchange for payment.

phishing An internet scam in which a user is deceived into providing personal or confidential information.

regulation The act or state of being subject to rules or orders issued by a government agency to provide legal oversight.

telecommunications Technology that deals with communications via radio, television, wire, satellite, and cable.

throttling The intentional slowing of network speed by an I.S.P.

tiered internet Internet service in which users may pay increasing fees for access to a greater number of services or products.

unfettered Unrestrained, free.

utility A service (such as electricity or water) provided by a public utility.

web A part of the internet accessible via a graphic interface and containing documents connected by hyperlinks.

zero-rating The practice of allowing internet users unlimited access to data to access specific websites or programs while limiting their data to access other websites or programs.

Media Literacy Terms

"Media literacy" refers to the ability to access, understand, critically assess and create media. The following terms are important components of media literacy, and they will help you critically engage with the articles in this title.

angle The aspect of a news story that a journalist focuses on and develops.

attribution The method by which a source is identified or by which facts and information are assigned to the person who provided them.

balance Principle of journalism that both perspectives of an argument should be presented in a fair way.

bias A disposition of prejudice in favor of a certain idea, person, or perspective.

byline Name of the writer, usually placed between the headline and the story.

chronological order Method of writing a story presenting the details of the story in the order in which they occurred.

credibility The quality of being trustworthy and believable, said of a journalistic source.

editorial Article of opinion or interpretation.

feature story Article designed to entertain as well as to inform.

headline Type, usually 18 point or larger, used to introduce a story.

human interest story Type of story that focuses on individuals and how events or issues affect their life, generally offering a sense of relatability to the reader.

impartiality Principle of journalism that a story should not reflect a journalist's bias and should contain balance.

intention The motive or reason behind something, such as the publication of a news story.

interview story Type of story in which the facts are gathered primarily by interviewing another person or persons.

inverted pyramid Method of writing a story using facts in order of importance, beginning with a lead and then gradually adding paragraphs in order of relevance from most interesting to least interesting.

motive The reason behind something, such as the publication of a news story or a source's perspective on an issue.

news story An article or style of expository writing that reports news, generally in a straightforward fashion and without editorial comment.

op-ed An opinion piece that reflects a prominent journalist's opinion on a topic of interest.

paraphrase The summary of an individual's words, with attribution, rather than a direct quotation of their exact words.

quotation The use of an individual's exact words indicated by the use of quotation marks and proper attribution.

reliability The quality of being dependable and accurate, said of a journalistic source.

rhetorical device Technique in writing intending to persuade the reader or communicate a message from a certain perspective.

tone A manner of expression in writing or speech.

Media Literacy Questions

1. "Tollbooths on the Internet Highway" (on page 16) is an example of an editorial. How is its byline different from other articles' bylines? What is the intention of this editorial?

2. "'Neutrality' Is New Challenge for Internet Pioneer" (on page 24) is an example of an interview. What is the value of being able to read Sir Tim Berners-Lee's quoted responses, as opposed to paraphrases? What purpose does John Markoff's introduction to the interview serve?

3. Does the article "Congress to Take Up Net's Future" (on page 29) demonstrate the journalistic principle of balance? How?

4. Compare the headlines of "Hey, Baby Bells: Information Still Wants to Be Free" (on page 10) and "Verizon Blocks Messages of Abortion Rights Group" (on page 32). What type of stories are these two articles? Compare their tone and style.

5. What is the tone of Joe Nocera's article "The Struggle for What We Already Have" (on page 68)? Can you identify ways in which he conveys that tone?

6. In "Rebuffing F.C.C. in 'Net Neutrality' Case, Court Allows Streaming Deals" (on page 83), Edward Wyatt quotes various sources. What is the benefit of using direct quotes? What is the benefit of using multiple sources?

7. "Defending the Open Internet" (on page 105) has three different parts. What is the intention of the article? How does each part contribute to that intention?

8. Identify the sources cited in the article "Net Neutrality Rules" (on page 134). How does Joe Nocera attribute information to each of these sources in their article? How effective are their attributions in helping the reader identify their sources?

9. W. Kamau Bell's "Net Neutrality: Why Artists and Activists Can't Afford to Lose It" (on page 171) is an example of an op-ed. Bell is a stand-up comic. How is Bell's profession relevant to his piece?

10. "F.C.C. Plan to Roll Back Net Neutrality Worries Small Businesses" (on page 174) is an example of a human interest story. What audience does this story appeal to? What techniques make the story relatable?

11. "How Repealing Net Neutrality Will Hurt Consumers" (on page 182) contains letters to the editor from members of the public. Compare the intention of each letter. How do their tones contrast?

12. "In Protests of Net Neutrality Repeal, Teenage Voices Stood Out" (on page 197) is another human interest story. What audience does it appeal to? How does it differ from "F.C.C. Plan to Roll Back Net Neutrality Worries Small Businesses" (on page 174)?

Citations

All citations in this list are formatted according to the Modern Language Association's (MLA) style guide.

BOOK CITATION

NEW YORK TIMES EDITORIAL STAFF, THE. *Net Neutrality: Seeking a Free and Fair Internet.* New York Times Educational Publishing, 2019.

ARTICLE CITATIONS

BELL, W. KAMAU. "Net Neutrality: Why Artists and Activists Can't Afford to Lose It." *The New York Times*, 31 Oct. 2017, https://www.nytimes.com/2017/10/31/opinion/net-neutrality-artists-activists.html.

BILTON, NICK. "Disruptions: Paying to Travel in the Internet's Fast Lanes." *The New York Times*, 2 Feb. 2014, https://bits.blogs.nytimes.com/2014/02/02/disruptions-paying-to-travel-in-the-internets-fast-lanes/.

CAIN MILLER, CLAIRE, AND BRIAN STELTER. "Web Plan Is Dividing Companies." *The New York Times*, 11 Aug. 2010, https://www.nytimes.com/2010/08/12/technology/12net.html.

CAIN MILLER, CLAIRE, AND MIGUEL HELFT. "Google Plan With Verizon Disillusions Some Allies." *The New York Times*, 15 Aug. 2010, https://www.nytimes.com/2010/08/16/technology/16google.html.

CAIN MILLER, CLAIRE, AND MIGUEL HELFT. "Web Plan From Google and Verizon Is Criticized." *The New York Times*, 9 Aug. 2010, https://www.nytimes.com/2010/08/10/technology/10net.html.

COHEN, ADAM. "Why the Democratic Ethic of the World Wide Web May Be About to End." *The New York Times*, 28 May 2006, http://www.nytimes.com/2006/05/28/opinion/28sun3.html.

ENGELHART, KEN. "Why Concerns About Net Neutrality Are Overblown." *The New York Times*, 4 Dec. 2017, https://www.nytimes.com/2017/12/04/opinion/net-neutrality-overblown-concerns.html.

HANSELL, SAUL. "F.C.C. Seeks to Protect Free Flow of Internet Data." *The New York Times*, 18 Sept. 2009, http://www.nytimes.com/2009/09/19/technology/internet/19net.html.

HANSELL, SAUL. "F.C.C. Vote Sets Precedent on Unfettered Web Usage." *The New York Times*, 2 Aug. 2008, https://www.nytimes.com/2008/08/02/technology/02fcc.html.

"How Repealing Net Neutrality Will Hurt Consumers." *The New York Times*, 29 Nov. 2017, https://www.nytimes.com/2017/11/29/opinion/net-neutrality-consumers.html.

HSU, TIFFANY. "F.C.C. Plan to Roll Back Net Neutrality Worries Small Businesses." *The New York Times*, 22 Nov. 2017, https://www.nytimes.com/2017/11/22/business/net-neutrality-small-businesses.html.

KANG, CECILIA. "Court Backs Rules Treating Internet as Utility, Not Luxury." *The New York Times*, 14 Jun. 2016, https://www.nytimes.com/2016/06/15/technology/net-neutrality-fcc-appeals-court-ruling.html.

KANG, CECILIA. "F.C.C. Chairman Pushes Sweeping Changes to Net Neutrality Rules." *The New York Times*, 26 Apr. 2017, https://www.nytimes.com/2017/04/26/technology/net-neutrality.html.

KANG, CECILIA. "F.C.C. Repeals Net Neutrality Rules." *The New York Times*, 14 Dec. 2017, https://www.nytimes.com/2017/12/14/technology/net-neutrality-repeal-vote.html.

KANG, CECILIA. "Flurry of Lawsuits Filed to Fight Repeal of Net Neutrality." *The New York Times*, 16 Jan. 2018, https://www.nytimes.com/2018/01/16/technology/net-neutrality-lawsuit-attorneys-general.html.

KANG, CECILIA. "In Protests of Net Neutrality Repeal, Teenage Voices Stood Out." *The New York Times*, 20 Dec. 2017, https://www.nytimes.com/2017/12/20/technology/net-neutrality-repeal-teens.html.

KANG, CECILIA. "Net Neutrality Hits a Nerve, Eliciting Intense Reactions." *The New York Times*, 28 Nov. 2017, https://www.nytimes.com/2017/11/28/technology/net-neutrality-reaction.html.

KANG, CECILIA. "States Push Back After Net Neutrality Repeal." *The New York Times*, 11 Jan. 2018, https://www.nytimes.com/2018/01/11/technology/net-neutrality-states.html.

KANG, CECILIA. "Trump's F.C.C. Pick Quickly Targets Net Neutrality Rules." *The New York Times*, 5 Feb. 2017, https://www.nytimes.com/2017/02/05/technology/trumps-fcc-quickly-targets-net-neutrality-rules.html.

KANG, CECILIA. "Washington Governor Signs First State Net Neutrality Bill."

The New York Times, 5 Mar. 2018, https://www.nytimes.com/2018/03/05/business/net-neutrality-washington-state.html.

KANG, CECILIA, DAISUKE WAKABAYASHI, NICK WINGFIELD, AND MIKE ISAAC. "Net Neutrality Protests Move Online, Yet Big Tech Is Quiet." *The New York Times*, 12 Dec. 2017, https://www.nytimes.com/2017/12/12/technology/net-neutrality-fcc-tech.html.

LABATON, STEPHEN. "Congress to Take Up Net's Future." *The New York Times*, 10 Jan. 2007, https://www.nytimes.com/2007/01/10/washington/10net.html.

LIPTAK, ADAM. "Verizon Blocks Messages of Abortion Rights Group." *The New York Times*, 27 Sept. 2007, https://www.nytimes.com/2007/09/27/us/27verizon.html.

LOHR, STEVE. "F.C.C. Dissenter Takes On Net Neutrality Proposal." *The New York Times*, 10 Feb. 2015, https://bits.blogs.nytimes.com/2015/02/10/f-c-c-dissenter-takes-on-net-neutrality-proposal/.

LOHR, STEVE. "F.C.C. Plans Strong Hand to Regulate the Internet." *The New York Times*, 4 Feb. 2015, https://www.nytimes.com/2015/02/05/technology/fcc-wheeler-net-neutrality.html.

LOHR, STEVE. "Internet Taxes, Another Window Into the Net Neutrality Debate." *The New York Times*, 20 Feb. 2015, https://bits.blogs.nytimes.com/2015/02/20/internet-taxes-another-window-into-the-net-neutrality-debate/.

MANJOO, FARHAD. "In Net Neutrality Push, Internet Giants on the Sidelines." *The New York Times*, 11 Nov. 2014, https://www.nytimes.com/2014/11/13/technology/in-net-neutrality-debate-tech-giants-on-the-sidelines.html.

MARKOFF, JOHN. "'Neutrality' Is New Challenge for Internet Pioneer." *The New York Times*, 27 Sept. 2006, https://www.nytimes.com/2006/09/27/technology/circuits/27neut.html.

MITCHELL, DAN. "No Neutral Ground in Net Debate." *The New York Times*, 13 May 2006, https://www.nytimes.com/2006/05/13/business/13online.html.

THE NEW YORK TIMES. "Mr. Obama's Internet Agenda." *The New York Times*, 15 Dec. 2008, https://www.nytimes.com/2008/12/16/opinion/16tue3.html.

THE NEW YORK TIMES. "Tollbooths on the Internet Highway." *The New York Times*, 20 Feb. 2006, https://www.nytimes.com/2006/02/20/opinion/tollbooths-on-the-internet-highway.html.

NOCERA, JOE. "Net Neutrality Rules." *The New York Times*, 6 Feb. 2015, https://www.nytimes.com/2015/02/07/opinion/joe-nocera-net-neutrality-rules.html.

NOCERA, JOE. "The Struggle for What We Already Have." *The New York Times*, 3 Sept. 2010, https://www.nytimes.com/2010/09/04/business/04nocera.html.

PORTER, EDUARDO. "Keeping the Internet Neutral." *The New York Times*, 8 May 2012, https://www.nytimes.com/2012/05/09/business/economy/net-neutrality-and-economic-equality-are-intertwined.html.

RAFF, ADAM. "Search, but You May Not Find." *The New York Times*, 27 Dec. 2009, https://www.nytimes.com/2009/12/28/opinion/28raff.html.

RUIZ, REBECCA R. "Congress Scrutinizes F.C.C. Following Release of New Internet Rules." *The New York Times*, 17 Mar. 2015, https://bits.blogs.nytimes.com/2015/03/17/congress-scrutinizes-f-c-c-following-release-of-new-internet-rules/.

RUIZ, REBECCA R. "Reaction to Regulation: 1934 vs. Today." *The New York Times*, 5 Mar. 2015, https://bits.blogs.nytimes.com/2015/03/05/reaction-to-regulation-1934-vs-today/.

RUIZ, REBECCA R., AND STEVE LOHR. "F.C.C. Approves Net Neutrality Rules, Classifying Broadband Internet Service as a Utility." *The New York Times*, 26 Feb. 2015, https://www.nytimes.com/2015/02/27/technology/net-neutrality-fcc-vote-internet-utility.html.

SOMMER, JEFF. "Defending the Open Internet." *The New York Times*, 10 May 2014, https://www.nytimes.com/2014/05/11/business/defending-the-open-internet.html.

STELTER, BRIAN. "F.C.C. Approves Net Rules and Braces for Fight." *The New York Times*, 21 Dec. 2010, https://mediadecoder.blogs.nytimes.com/2010/12/21/f-c-c-approves-net-rules-and-braces-for-fight/.

STEWART, JAMES B. "How Netflix Keeps Finding Itself on the Same Side as Regulators." *The New York Times*, 28 May 2015, https://www.nytimes.com/2015/05/29/business/media/how-netflix-keeps-finding-itself-on-the-same-side-as-regulators.html.

STROSS, RANDALL. "Hey, Baby Bells: Information Still Wants to Be Free." *The New York Times*, 15 Jan. 2006, https://www.nytimes.com/2006/01/15/business/yourmoney/hey-baby-bells-information-still-wants-to-be-free.html.

WYATT, EDWARD. "F.C.C., in a Shift, Backs Fast Lanes for Web Traffic." *The New York Times*, 23 Apr. 2014, https://www.nytimes.com/2014/04/24/technology/fcc-new-net-neutrality-rules.html.

WYATT, EDWARD. "F.C.C. Proposes Rules on Internet Access." *The New York Times*, 6 May 2010, https://www.nytimes.com/2010/05/07/technology/

07broadband.html.

WYATT, EDWARD. "F.C.C. Seeks a New Path on 'Net Neutrality' Rules." *The New York Times*, 19 Feb. 2014, https://www.nytimes.com/2014/02/20/business/fcc-to-propose-new-rules-on-open-internet.html.

WYATT, EDWARD. "House Votes Against 'Net Neutrality.'" *The New York Times*, 8 Apr. 2011, https://www.nytimes.com/2011/04/09/business/media/09broadband.html.

WYATT, EDWARD. "Lawmakers Introduce Bill to Ban Paid Prioritization." *The New York Times*, 17 June 2014, https://bits.blogs.nytimes.com/2014/06/17/lawmakers-introduce-bill-to-ban-paid-prioritization/.

WYATT, EDWARD. "Obama and Scalia, United on Broadband as a Utility." *The New York Times*, 13 Nov. 2014, https://bits.blogs.nytimes.com/2014/11/13/obama-and-scalia-united-on-broadband-as-a-utility/.

WYATT, EDWARD. "Obama Asks F.C.C. to Adopt Tough Net Neutrality Rules." *The New York Times*, 10 Nov. 2014, https://www.nytimes.com/2014/11/11/technology/obama-net-neutrality-fcc.html.

WYATT, EDWARD. "Obama's Net Neutrality Bid Divides Civil Rights Groups." *The New York Times*, 7 Dec. 2014, https://www.nytimes.com/2014/12/08/business/obamas-net-neutrality-bid-divides-civil-rights-groups.html.

WYATT, EDWARD. "Rebuffing F.C.C. in 'Net Neutrality' Case, Court Allows Streaming Deals." *The New York Times*, 14 Jan. 2014, https://www.nytimes.com/2014/01/15/technology/appeals-court-rejects-fcc-rules-on-internet-service-providers.html.

WYATT, EDWARD. "Top Cable Lobbyist Argues Against Broadband as Utility." *The New York Times*, 29 Apr. 2014, https://bits.blogs.nytimes.com/2014/04/29/top-cable-lobbyist-argues-against-broadband-as-utility/.

WYATT, EDWARD. "U.S. Court Curbs F.C.C. Authority on Web Traffic." *The New York Times*, 6 Apr. 2010, https://www.nytimes.com/2010/04/07/technology/07net.html.

WYATT, EDWARD, AND NOAM COHEN. "Comcast and Netflix Reach Deal on Service." *The New York Times*, 23 Feb. 2014, https://www.nytimes.com/2014/02/24/business/media/comcast-and-netflix-reach-a-streaming-agreement.html.

Index

W

Y

Z